THE DOG DECODER

Brimming with creative inspiration, how-to projects, and useful information to enrich your everyday life, Quarto Knows is a favorite destination for those pursuing their interests and passions. Visit our site and dig deeper with our books into your area of interest: Quarto Creates, Quarto Cooks, Quarto Homes, Quarto Lives, Quarto Drives, Quarto Explores, Quarto Gifts, or Quarto Kids.

A QUARTO BOOK

This edition published in 2018 by Chartwell Books,
an imprint of The Quarto Group
142 West 36th Street, 4th Floor
New York, NY 10018 USA
T (212) 779-4972 F (212) 779-6058
www.QuartoKnows.com

ISBN: 978-0-7858-3629-2

QUAR: M DGD

Conceived, edited, and designed by
Quarto Publishing plc
an imprint of The Quarto Group
The Old Brewery
6 Blundell Street
London N7 9BH

Chartwell Books titles are also available at discount for retail, wholesale, promotional, and bulk purchase. For details, contact the Special Sales Manager by email at specialsales@quarto.com or by mail at The Quarto Group, Attn: Special Sales Manager, 401 Second Avenue North, Suite 310, Minneapolis, MN 55401, USA.

10 9 8 7 6 5 4 3 2 1

Printed in China

MIX
Paper from responsible sources
FSC® C104723

No animals were put in danger or hurt in the photography used in this book.

THE DOG DECODER

The Essential Guide
to Understanding
Your Dog's Behavior

DAVID ALDERTON

CHARTWELL
BOOKS

Contents

Special Skills   132
All kinds of dogs with special attributes

Introduction

Many owners lament the fact that their dogs cannot talk, but if you look a bit deeper into your relationship with your pet, you will soon recognize the key signs revealing that your dog is actually engaging in an ongoing conversation with you.

Defining the relationship

As a species, we rely very heavily on verbal communication, having developed complex linguistic skills, but this has skewed our ability to communicate in other, more subtle ways. When it comes to receiving information, we rely to a great extent on our observational powers. Domestic dogs, in contrast, take a more balanced, broader view of the world around them. Just like their ancestor, the gray wolf and indeed all wild canids, they will build up a recent history of their environment at the same time as they communicate with each other, due to their acute sense of smell.

The scenting powers of dogs are far more effective than our own, and their hearing is superior, too. As a result, this lessens their reliance on their sense of sight. In fact, an elderly dog that loses its sight is usually able to manage pretty well, in a way that would be impossible for a blind person. Dogs even have specialized, thickened, and elongated sensory hairs in the guise of whiskers above their eyes, on the sides on their heads, and on their chins. These help them find their way at close quarters.

The bond that has developed between dog and human is unique throughout the animal kingdom, and it is easy to identify how this has come about, to mutual benefit. Dogs have aided people in numerous ways in the past and continue to enrich our lives today. Their relationship with people has evolved to the extent that, now, they can even be trained for medical purposes, to sniff out potentially deadly cancers and to save lives.

Dogs such as this young Border Collie are highly valued as working companions because of their specialist skills.

Cavalier King Charles Spaniels are one of today's most popular breeds.

Individual nature

Dogs are very adept at attracting our attention in a wide range of ways, starting with their appearance. Many breeds, especially smaller dogs, look cute and immediately appeal to us. Every dog is an individual, though—even in the case of purebreds—and this unique aspect to their character reinforces the appeal of dogs as companions, irrespective of their looks.

Breed awareness

One of the most amazing features of the domestic dog today is the diversity in size and form that exists— aside from other characteristics, such as coat length and coloration—with around 400 distinctive breeds occurring worldwide. A number of these are still kept for working purposes, such as herding cattle, locating truffles (a valuable form of fungi) underground, or simply acting as guardians.

The ways in which they communicate may superficially appear similar—in as much as they bark, perhaps, or may scratch—but breed-specific behavior, relating to the individual's past, can clearly be identified in many cases. This tends to reflect the environment where, and the purpose for which, the breed was originally created. But a breed's appearance is not static, and some have changed quite dramatically in appearance over the years.

Yorkshire Terriers have a tough, working ancestry but are now kept essentially as pets.

The unwritten dialogue

By observing your dog's behavior, you will be able to learn a great deal about what it is thinking, feeling, and even intending to do. A dog will also be able to indicate to you when it wants to go out, is eager to play, or if it is feeling sick. By understanding what it is saying, you will enjoy a much closer relationship with your pet.

The English Bulldog is a very distinctive breed that is characterized by its large, broad head.

Drinking   Jumping

Greetings

Rolling
over

Excitement

Resting

At Home with Your Dog

Day-to-day routines and activities

Scratching

Begging

Seeking attention

Vocalization

Visitors

Play

Stealing food

Sleeping

Strangers

Resting

It is quite usual for adult dogs to rest (but not necessarily sleep) for long periods during the day, although your particular domestic routine will influence this aspect of your pet's behavior. Puppies, on the other hand, will run around and play energetically and then just stop, going to sleep almost immediately.

The morning rest routine

Your dog will be active in the morning, waking up and looking forward to a walk, as well as its breakfast. After exercise and a meal, your pet will become sleepy, though, and will settle down for a while. You should always feed a dog when it is ready to rest, rather than before taking it for a run. Otherwise it is vulnerable to gastric torsion (or bloat), where the stomach becomes twisted—a potentially life-threatening condition.

Resting location Dogs will rest in a variety of locations, sometimes just lying on the floor by your feet if you are sitting down, like this Yorkshire Terrier, although they are unlikely to sleep properly there. They will prefer to seek out a bed or sofa for this purpose.

Still alert Your resting dog will still clearly be awake, watching what is going on and ready to pick up on any smells or sounds that catch its attention. It may follow you if you move elsewhere.

Patient position

Once your resting dog detects something of possible interest, it is likely to sit up and look at what is happening before deciding what to do next. Alternatively, it may leap up onto its feet immediately and head off elsewhere. The resting posture reflects a patient approach, as the dog waits for something to happen. Most dogs do not like to sit for long, but they will lie down in this way for extended periods.

Ready for action A resting dog will tend to lie in this posture, with its front legs extended. The dog can regain its feet from this position very quickly. At this stage, though, it is still deciding whether to simply watch or become involved in what is happening.

Ears This resting Miniature Schnauzer is following what is going on with its eyes; the position of the ears also indicates that it is alert, but not concerned. Its ears are slightly raised, and held away from the head.

SAFETY FIRST

If your dog starts to sleep for longer than usual and loses interest in food, these are typical signs of illness— seek veterinary advice.

Wild trait

Resting behavior, as described here, is commonly seen in wild dogs as well as Gray Wolves. In their natural habitats, wild dogs spend much of their time lying around, not sleeping but on the lookout for likely hunting opportunities or possible danger. Lying down has the additional advantage of helping to conceal the dogs' presence in an area because it makes them less conspicuous. This is not just the case in grassland areas, but in more open, sandy terrain as well, where their coloration provides camouflage.

Sleeping

One of the characteristics of domestic dogs is that they will sleep for relatively long periods, not just at night but throughout the day as well. This is a reflection of the behavior of their wild ancestors.

Making the bed

Domestic dogs sleep in a way identical to wolves. Although your pet may be using a dog bed, it will still typically walk around in a tight circle before settling down to sleep. In the wild, this would help flatten plants, providing a more comfortable sleeping area. Curling up in vegetation when possible, rather than being in the open, helps to keep the wild dog or wolf hidden while asleep and unable to defend itself.

Why so much sleep?

In common with other predatory species, wild dogs spend much of the day asleep. This may be related to their feeding habits. Unlike herbivores—which eat plants that have a low nutritional value and so have to feed for much of the day to obtain sufficient nutrients—dogs benefit from a concentrated diet consisting largely of meat, which meets all their energy requirements in a more efficient way. As a result, they can sleep for long periods whenever they are not hunting. Once they have eaten, after the exertion of hunting and overpowering their quarry, they settle down to sleep once more. This behavior is mimicked by domestic dogs that come back after a walk and feed before falling asleep soon afterward.

Curled up tight Wolves sleep in this position to help conserve body heat, and to keep snow from blowing into their faces. Domestic dogs still like to sleep in the same position as their wild ancestors.

The daily sleep routine

Domestic dogs soon develop set times for sleeping as part of their daily routine, although this may be influenced to some extent by the weather and the time of year. When the weather is bad, they may display less interest in going out and so sleep for longer. If there is the opportunity to go out with you, your pet is likely to wake up immediately and will be eager to venture outdoors for any unexpected walk. Age also plays a part, with dogs tending to sleep for longer periods as they get older.

Comfortable sleep
Pet dogs often stretch out when they are asleep, and a bean bag may be more comfortable for them than a rigid dog's bed.

Dreaming

Dogs start their sleep curled up in a ball as described, but then they will often stretch out onto their sides, especially in warm indoor surroundings. It is relatively common for them to show signs of dreaming. Your dog may start twitching and even go through a series of running movements with its legs. This does not happen on every occasion that a dog falls asleep, but these signals are an indicator that the dog has entered a phase of so-called "REM" (rapid eye movement) sleep. This is a type of sleep that is almost like being awake, when the eyes, although closed, are moving—and it seems to be when dreams occur.

Let sleeping dogs lie It is not a good idea to rouse a sleeping dog by suddenly touching it, because it may react aggressively to being awakened in this way. Your pet will generally wake up quickly if called.

Snoring Some types of dog, such as this Mastiff, are more likely to snore than others.

Scratching

Scratching behavior in a dog can take a number of different forms, and has a variety of purposes. Dogs may scratch themselves as part of the grooming process, but they will also use their claws in a similar way on items in their environment.

Fleas

One of the most common causes of scratching is the presence of fleas in the dog's coat. They tend to be more prevalent during the warmer months of the year. It is not the flea itself that triggers the scratching behavior, but rather its feeding habits. These parasites feed on the blood of their host, using their sharp mouth parts to break through the skin before injecting a tiny quantity of their saliva into the tissue. It is the saliva that causes the irritation, and it can result in a dog scratching very intensively, sometimes even injuring itself. This type of reaction is especially likely if the dog has developed an allergy to the flea's saliva.

By any means
Dogs may use their front or hind legs to scratch themselves, depending on where the source of the irritation is and the easiest way to reach it.

Other causes of scratching

While all dogs scratch themselves occasionally, frequent scratching may indicate an underlying health problem. Fleas are not the only possible cause—food intolerances and allergies may also elicit similar signs. A dog that is suffering from severe skin irritation will not just scratch, but is also likely to nibble intently at its coat. And if the dog is caught doing something wrong, it may also start scratching itself as a diversionary tactic.

Diggers Terriers were bred to dig small animals out of burrows.

Scraping and digging

All dogs—especially unneutered male dogs—will deliberately scratch, or "scrape," the ground after urination. This involves the dog taking its weight on its front legs and scratching with each hind leg in turn—this is done with sufficient force to uproot any grass in the area. The dog's sweat glands are located between the toes, and by performing this action it leaves behind its individual scent, marking its territory.

Terriers in particular will use their claws not just for scratching at the surface but also digging into the ground. They may do this if they detect the burrow of a rat or fox, whereas other dogs may also dig down with the purpose of burying a bone or similar edible item. This is something that wild dogs do, as a means of hiding, or "caching," the remains of a meal out of sight of scavengers, with the intention of finishing it later.

Ear infection Seek veterinary advice without delay, if repeated, prolonged bouts of ear scratching occur. Such behavior indicates an infection, which can have serious consequences if left untreated, causing permanent damage and even deafness.

Normal scratching Dogs will use their claws to scratch their bodies quite regularly. This is part of their grooming process, helping them to cope with itchy skin and possibly also to break down any matted areas that may be forming in their coat.

Never too young Even young puppies, such as this Beagle, can acquire fleas.

Drinking

The amount of water that a dog drinks will be influenced by various factors, including its level of activity and the temperature outside. Its diet, too, will play a part, simply because dry food—as its name suggests—contains far less water than fresh food or that sold in pouches or cans.

STOPPING TO DRINK
When out for a walk, especially on a warm day, dogs will tend to stop frequently to drink from puddles, or larger bodies of water such as rivers. If possible, carry water with you to avoid the risk of your dog consuming algae or other pollutants.

Chlorine detection

In spite of your attempts to provide your dog with a fresh, clean supply of drinking water, you may be discouraged to find that it drinks elsewhere at every opportunity. Even so, it is still important to keep providing fresh water every day. When a dog wants to drink from its water bowl, it will do so; why it may prefer to drink elsewhere is unclear. It is possible that the chlorine-based compounds added to water from the faucet to make it safe for human consumption are distasteful to dogs, with their highly developed sense of smell. Chlorine gas can be a severe respiratory irritant and, when water containing it is left standing, it will come out of solution over the course of several days. Dogs may detect this gas when they are lapping up the water.

Drinking from the toilet

An aversion to harmful chemicals may not be enough to keep larger dogs from drinking out of the toilet, where other more dangerous chemicals such as bleach are likely to also be present. This habit is also extremely unhygienic. The behavior tends to start in puppyhood and should be prevented. The solution is simple: keep your dog out of the bathroom, and keep the toilet lid closed as a secondary precaution.

A dangerous habit
Drinking from the toilet could make your dog very sick. Prevent this by keeping the toilet lid closed at all times.

Algae hazard

You cannot assume that water from "natural" sources is necessarily safe for your dog, especially in hot weather when there is an algal bloom, which may have turned the water greenish. Certain algae are toxic to dogs, and can kill them within an hour if no treatment is given. Dogs do not appear to recognize the danger posed by algal blooms. Sudden profuse salivation and pale gums are warning signs that must be taken seriously, even if the water you passed did not appear discolored. If you notice these symptoms after a walk near water, consult your vet immediately.

Clean water wherever you are

If you are going out hiking any distance with your pet, be sure to take a bottle of water and a bowl with you, so your dog has the opportunity to drink whenever it becomes thirsty. Well-designed, convenient travel packs are available for use under these circumstances. You can also buy water that contains electrolytes as a way of maintaining the natural chemical balance within your dog's body during or after a period of exercise.

At home, some dog owners offer their pets filtered water, believing this to be a better option than using water fresh from the faucet. Although filters designed for humans can be used, at least one major pet supplies manufacturer now offers a combined filter-and-drinking-bowl system specifically for dogs. However, do bear in mind that a dog's drinking preferences may be set early in life. If you offer filtered water, your pet may then be disinclined to drink water from the faucet.

Water only

Some owners like to offer their dogs milk to drink, in addition to water. Unfortunately, not all dogs possess the essential lactase enzymes needed to break down the milk sugar, lactose. Consequently the dog suffers an upset stomach, with the undigested milk fermenting in the gut. The end result is likely to be increased flatulence—uncomfortable for the dog and unpleasant for you. Dogs eating a balanced diet do not require any milk—only water.

TIP

- *Dogs find it easier to drink from a relatively large water bowl.*

Not tasty?
In spite of it being clean, many dogs do not seem to like the taste of water from the faucet, and prefer other sources.

Hot-weather drinking
All breeds of dog pant to keep cool in hot weather, and in doing so lose water. This is why dogs (just like us, who sweat the water out) need to drink more during periods of hot weather.

SAFETY FIRST

Harmful bacteria can multiply rapidly in a dog's water bowl, especially if there are any food particles in it. Make sure you wash it regularly.

Begging

Although it is often said that dogs are trained by us, the reality is rather different. In fact, dogs have the ability to influence our actions through their behavior. At no time is this more evident than when they ask for food; they have developed a range of tactics for the purpose of attracting our attention.

Stay in charge Don't allow your meals to become disrupted by your dog staring longingly at your food. Under no circumstances should you feed your dog food from the table.

Time to eat

As creatures of routine, dogs instinctively know when it is time to eat, just as they know when it is time to go out for a walk. They do not need a clock for this purpose, and if you are late in providing food, you will be reminded! At first, the hungry dog will become noticeably restless. If ignored, it is then likely to start pawing you gently—a habit common in larger dogs. Smaller dogs may become more lively and are more likely to bark excitedly and repeatedly.

Risk of overfeeding Your dog may try to convince you that it is still hungry, even if it has had the recommended amount of food already that day. Some breeds of dogs, such as Golden Retrievers, are naturally greedier than others, and this means they are at greater risk of becoming obese.

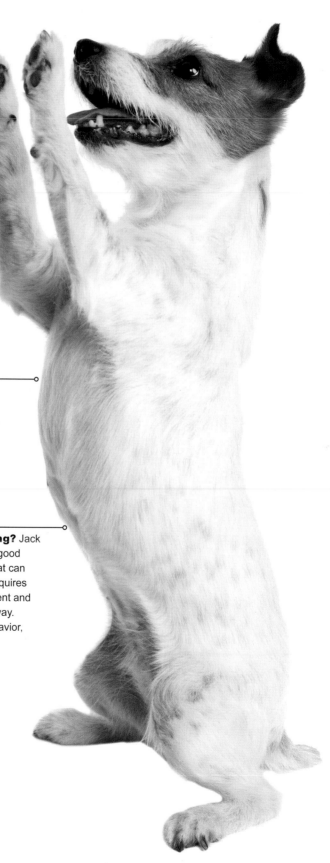

Communication methods

The size of your dog will directly impact the way that it communicates its growing hunger to you. A large dog, such as a Golden Retriever, is able to give its bowl to you, whereas small breeds will tend to become more excited and possibly try to jump up onto your lap, without settling down there. Instead, when you move, they will leap down and run off in the direction of their food bowl to show you what they want.

Getting vocal

Dogs soon come to recognize that they need to persuade you to look in their direction, whatever it is they want. While a large dog can simply place a paw on your leg when you are sitting down, it can be harder for smaller dogs to gain your attention. This may help to explain why smaller dogs tend to be more vocal than larger dogs. Yapping is an efficient—if irritating—way to attract your attention.

Attention grabbing Jack Russell Terriers have a compact body shape and are adept at supporting themselves in an upright position—and when they see that this type of begging behavior attracts praise or attention from their owner, they will repeat it.

SAFETY FIRST

Do not get into the habit of offering treats to your dog when it begs—otherwise it will soon become overweight.

Training or begging? Jack Russell Terriers are a good example of a breed that can be hard to train and requires plenty of encouragement and food treats along the way. Only reward good behavior, though—not begging.

Reinforced behavior

Begging is a learned behavior, rather than being instinctive. Not all dogs of the same breed behave in the same way, and begging tends to be a skill that is acquired at an early stage in life. This "skill" will soon become habit if you always respond to your dog when it begs; your response reinforces its behavior.

Stealing food

It can be very irritating, but all dogs will steal food, especially if there is no one around at the time and they can do so undetected. Therefore, be sure to keep all edible items out of your dog's reach, so your pet will not be tempted.

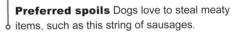

Forbidden treats

The underlying reason for stealing food is usually not actual hunger. It is likely the simple fact that forbidden food is more appealing, even if it is not as healthy as the careful diet that you normally offer your pet. Meat or meat-based items are especially appealing to dogs; apples, for example, are likely to be ignored.

Preferred spoils Dogs love to steal meaty items, such as this string of sausages.

Ancestral explanations

Gray wolves tend to be opportunistic in their feeding habits; that's how they survive. If large prey is not available, they will subsist on small quarry, such as rodents. Furthermore, a subordinate individual may take food from a more dominant member that has seemingly stopped eating and wandered away. Domestic dogs have retained this sense that it is important to eat any food they find quickly, before they are detected with it and have it taken away.

TIP

Once a dog has learned a way of stealing food, it will likely do so again in the future—so a cupboard that has been raided once may need a latch installed.

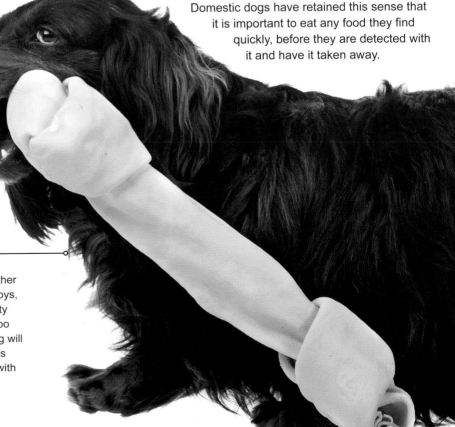

Hard to swallow It is not just food that is vulnerable—other "edible" items, such as chews or toys, may also be stolen if an opportunity presents itself. Where an item is too large to be swallowed easily, a dog will simply drag or carry it away, as this Long-haired Dachshund is doing with a large dog chew.

Bad habits

Dogs are more likely to steal food if they are fed tidbits on a regular basis, rather than just being offered food at set mealtimes, because they are then on the lookout for food throughout the day. They may take food directly off a table, or even learn to jump onto a nearby chair.

SAFETY FIRST

A number of human foods, including chocolate, are dangerous for dogs—the best advice is to keep all your food out of reach at all times.

Sneaking around

Having stolen food, your dog is most likely to disappear quickly with it, rather than remaining at the scene of the crime. It will retreat to an area where it is relatively well concealed from your view, perhaps behind a chair or in a different room. In typical canine style, it will then gulp the food down as quickly as possible, especially if it was able to carry it all away. If not, it is likely to remain closer to the original food source, hoping to have the opportunity to return and steal more.

Dangerous foods
Avoid leaving food on low tables, where even small breeds such as this Jack Russell Terrier can reach it. Dogs are especially at risk from eating chocolate in any form (such as candy bars and cookies)—it is toxic to them.

Signs of remorse

If caught in the act of stealing—or especially of eating—the food, your dog will seek to appease you, especially when scolded about its behavior. It will lower its ears and tail, wagging it from side to side in an act of contrition. Should you not discover the loss until much later, though, having given your dog the opportunity to eat the stolen food, then it will not act in this way, having already forgotten the event.

Seeking attention

Dogs love to interact with their owners and will often actively seek you out, jumping up to be stroked, for example. They soon learn by observation and repetition what the most effective means of attracting and holding your attention are.

Desperate to reach you

If your dog is outside or in another part of the house and cannot get to you, the most likely way that it will try to make its presence known is by barking. This tends to be just a couple of barks in quick succession, as opposed to the more intense repeated barking that you may hear when your dog has detected the approach of a stranger—or the repetitive, short barks that indicate excitement. In addition, however, the dog may scratch at a door with its claws, trying to open it, and it may also scratch the adjacent carpet or wooden flooring. Clearly, this is undesirable, so try not to leave your dog confined in a room away from you.

Different strategies

Smaller dogs are at a disadvantage in terms of their height when trying to catch your attention. But they can usually manage to jump up to you easily, especially if you are sitting down, possibly distracting you from what you are doing. Another method a dog will use to persuade you to acknowledge its presence is to start whining. This is a very different and quieter call note from a bark, but unmistakable at close quarters, and it will be uttered repeatedly. This is a indicator of frustration and demands attention.

Reaching up This small Terrier is doing its best to gain its owner's attention by standing up on its hind legs, but it may need to resort to other methods, too, in order to be successful.

Home alone

Dogs left on their own for long periods without attention may start to bark persistently. This can be a particular problem with an adopted dog, that its new owner may not even be aware of...until the neighbors complain about the noise. It then becomes a matter of reassurance, convincing the new dog that it will not be abandoned. Exercising your pet just before going out, so that it will be tired and settle down to sleep, may help, as can varying the length of your absence, sometimes just going out for a short period.

Opening doors

Dogs learn to employ a range of different methods when seeking your attention. They will watch how you act and can learn by example. For instance, if you have interior doors that open by pushing down the handles, some larger dogs may learn to master this technique.

More commonly, though, a dog will use one of its front paws in conjunction with its nose to get out of a room and join you elsewhere in the house. Assuming that the door is slightly ajar, it will place one of its front paws at the bottom of the door where it opens, and gently push it back. It will then use its nose higher up, to open the door and slip through the resulting gap. Your pet will then run out and come to find you. Not all dogs master this method of door-opening, though, and such behavior is not seen in young puppies, as they may not be strong enough.

Useful paws Some dogs are able to use their paws like hands, helping them open doors. They can also use them to scratch objects and furnishings to attract attention and try to reach you.

Built to escape Taller dogs have a distinct advantage when it comes to opening doors, as do those with relatively long, narrow noses, such as this cross-bred Spaniel.

Rolling over

The body of a dog may not be quite as flexible as that of a cat in terms of its anatomical structure, but dogs are still remarkably athletic in most cases, able not just to run and jump but also to curl up and roll over.

Why roll?

As with many other aspects of a dog's body language, there is no single explanation for why a dog will roll over. The context is very important in terms of understanding this behavior. Young puppies often adopt a rolling-over posture when they are play-fighting with a littermate. As far as a dog is concerned, this tends to be a submissive posture, exposing the vulnerable throat region to attack. Once a dog adopts this posture with its owner, however, it has a subtly different meaning. It becomes a sign of trust, with the dog asking to be stroked on its underparts. Puppies learn from an early age that by adopting this posture, they are likely to be given attention.

SAFETY FIRST

If you detect unexplained lumps on your dog's underside, seek veterinary advice—bitches especially can suffer from mammary tumors.

Playful pose This Labrador Retriever is lying on its back, paddling at its owner with its front paws—just asking for affection.

Stretching out This Cocker Spaniel is rolling after waking up to stretch itself.

A relaxed position

One reason that a dog may roll over is related to its body temperature. At first, a dog will generally curl up in a ball to go to sleep, with its head touching its tail. This behavior is not only seen in domestic dogs, but also in all their wild relatives. As the dog becomes warmer, however, it will stretch out, allowing heat trapped close to its body to dissipate. Eventually, the sleeping dog may roll over onto its back, especially if the surroundings are relatively comfortable.

Wake-up roll

When a dog wakes up, even if it has not been sleeping on its back as described above, it may choose to roll over. This flexes the long muscles of the back, similar to a person stretching after getting out of bed. Such behavior is less common in elderly dogs. They tend to stretch out on their sides when asleep; their bodies are less supple, making them unlikely to roll onto their backs.

Unpleasant habit Often, dogs such as this Bernese Mountain Dog will roll in excrement, perhaps to take on the scent of another animal.

Scent masking

A less welcome reason for a dog to roll is that it may choose to coat itself in the excrement of another animal, such as a cow, sheep, or fox. This is most common after a dog has been bathed. The reason is unclear, but it is thought to be related to the dog's social standing. Wild dogs do sometimes roll in the excrement of herbivores, and it is thought this may be a way of masking their own scent, allowing them to get closer to their quarry. In the case of a domestic dog, bathe your pet afterward and avoid exercising it in areas where it could easily soil its coat again for a couple of weeks. Otherwise, almost inevitably, your dog will attempt to behave in a similar way at the earliest opportunity.

Excitement

Dogs are naturally enthusiastic companions, always eager to go for a walk or take part in a game. This is a critical consideration as far as their training is concerned because, being eager to please you, they will respond best to positive encouragement.

Expressing excitement

Some dogs are more demonstrative than others when expressing excitement, and this is related to some extent to their physical appearance. Relatively athletic breeds are better suited to behaving in an excitable way than those with more corpulent bodies, such as Pugs. Young dogs in particular can easily become excited, and it might be necessary to calm them down. This is most likely as you are about to take your dog out for a walk, when it starts jumping up before you can attach the leash to its collar. Not only does this make the process difficult, but you might end up being knocked over. It is really important to be firm with a puppy when it does this, because—especially in the case of larger breeds—the problem can only get bigger! Equally, be sure that your dog does not pull you along on its leash in excitement, and that you are in control.

Excited barking A dog may show its excitement by barking repeatedly in short bursts. The particular position of the ears (depending on the breed) will indicate that your dog is in a lively mood.

On the move When an excited dog runs, other signs of excitement will be less apparent. Depending on whether they are carrying an object or not, they may bark repeatedly while on the move.

Back to basics When excited, dogs may revert to their working instincts; for instance, Poodles and other water breeds may plunge into a nearby lake.

SAFETY FIRST

Dogs are not likely to be aware of danger when they are excited. Carrying a stick can be especially dangerous if they stumble, as it could cause injury to the inside of the mouth or another part of the body.

Exciting play

Outdoors, the excitement will continue if your dog is running and chasing after toys, such as in a game of fetch. This is a great opportunity to build the bond between you. Some breeds—especially Retrievers— are instinctively more inclined to behave in this way, although any dog may potentially do so. The key thing is that the dog will need to have been taught to do this from puppyhood; older dogs do not master the art of playing in this way as enthusiastically. Once a dog has learned this pattern of behavior, however, it will still show the same degree of excitement whenever it has the opportunity to play like this. Dogs have very good memories and, especially if you repeat the game regularly, you are likely to find that before long, your dog will be trying to persuade you to play and will deliberately bring a toy to you for this purpose. See pages 32–33 for more on play.

Periods of calm

When a dog is excited, it is less likely than usual to respond to commands, being more inclined to concentrate on the game rather than on your instructions. It is therefore useful to stop playing at times, so that you can get the dog to calm down and focus on what you are saying. This is important because, when excited, a dog is likely to run off with its ball or toy and will not be as focused on what is happening around it. This may result in a dog running across a street, or slipping, for example. If you are concerned, never chase after your dog. It will see this as an extension of the game, and that you— as a fellow pack member—are running with it. It will not stop as required. If you stand still and turn your back as if about to head in the opposite direction, the dog will be less inclined to run off on its own and should calm down.

Lively nature If given the opportunity, dogs that are naturally agile usually respond when they are excited by running, leaping, and jumping.

Jumping

Some types of dogs are naturally more athletic than others, and this is reflected in their appearance. Relatively slim, long-legged individuals, such as Border Collies, can jump much more effectively than stocky, short-legged dogs such as Bulldogs.

Rudder The tail helps to steer the Border Collie, being held in a horizontal position at first, before being raised vertically as it leaps upward. The tail is generally at its highest point as the dog clears the barrier and is then lowered as the dog descends.

Up and over The dog keeps its front legs tucked under its body as it takes off, but then, as it reaches the top of its jump, it extends its legs forward.

Take-off The collie extends its body as it starts to lift off from the ground, with a clear view of what it is jumping over. This allows it to judge its position and avoid any risk of collision. At this stage, the front feet are tucked underneath the body.

Ready to go Powerful, muscular hindquarters provide the propulsive power for this Border Collie to gain momentum and lift itself off the ground. A dog leaps like a spring, transferring weight to its hindquarters before taking off.

Smooth landing As the dog nears the ground again, it reaches out to touch down first with its front feet, which absorb the initial impact, and then with its hind feet. This leaves it ready to bound off again quickly, as necessary.

Escape artists

Dogs will jump fences for a variety of reasons (see the illustration of a jumping dog opposite), possibly because there is food in a neighboring backyard or because they detect potential quarry, such as a fox. Another common reason for dogs to escape by jumping is when there is a bitch in heat nearby (see pages 60–61). She gives off chemical messengers called pheromones, which are carried on the wind and attract all the male dogs in the area. Neutering a male dog should help to decrease its desire to jump out of your property to reach a nearby female in heat.

Vertical leaps

Some dogs are naturally more athletic than others, with Jack Russell Terriers, in particular, able to jump very well. Their compact body shape and well-muscled hindquarters mean that they can even leap vertically without difficulty, for example, when catching a frisbee or a ball thrown into the air. This is a reflection of their ancestry as hunting companions. Their short legs precluded these Terriers from keeping up with the hounds when they were following a scent, so they accompanied the huntsmen instead, in case they were needed to drive a fox out of its burrow at a later stage. An individual needed to be agile enough to leap directly off the ground to be caught and carried by a rider, without the need to dismount. Dogs have been known to jump as high as 5½ ft. (1.73 m), so your backyard fencing must be high enough to keep your pet safely confined on your property.

Small but springy
Small dogs, such as this Jack Russell Terrier, are often very agile jumpers, and have the ability to spring up almost vertically.

AGILITY CONTESTS

Agility events require dogs to compete around an obstacle course, encouraged by their owners to climb, jump, and weave through various apparatus. The contests are open to all types of dogs, and size offers no guarantee of success.

Avoiding hazards

Dogs tend to be more inclined to jump when left to their own devices in the backyard. When out walking, your dog will usually be happy to accompany you through gates, rather than trying to jump hedges and fences, simply because it is following your example. Do not encourage your dog to jump over barriers in this environment, because it could end up injuring itself badly if it then tries to leap unsuccessfully over a barbed wire fence. The problem is that dogs do not appreciate the danger of injury under these circumstances, although they will be less inclined to jump as they grow older.

Vocalization

Dogs communicate their moods and intentions by their vocalizations, and although barking is the most common, they also possess a much more complex vocabulary of sounds, ranging from quiet chattering through whining to growling. Puppies, too, have a different and distinctive range of calls.

Whining

Young puppies are able to communicate vocally soon after birth by whining. This is a relatively quiet sound that will not be audible over a long distance, but its intensity is significant. Frequent, repetitive whining is indicative that something is wrong. The puppy may be too cold, for example, or it may be hungry, which, in turn, could indicate a health problem. Dogs may choose to continue whining as they grow older, as this frequently proves to be an effective means of communicating with their owners.

Watching for a reaction When whining, a dog will often raise its head, partly to see whether it has succeeded in attracting your attention.

Growling

This is a very distinctive sound which varies in intensity. It is a definite warning and should be heeded as such. A dog that is especially possessive by nature may growl if you try to take an object away from it, or it may growl in warning to another dog, as a prelude to a fight.

Talking

Some dogs will actually engage in a "conversation" with you at close quarters; more an expression of excitement than whining, with its more monotonous tone. This "talking behavior" is a call for recognition, and is often uttered following the initial excitement of your return home. It does not usually last long, and is often accompanied by your pet brushing against you at the same time to seek attention, rather than wanting to be fed or taken out for a walk—both typically triggers for whining in older dogs.

Tail talk A dog may not use its tail if sitting and barking, but if it is standing, it will reinforce its message by gesturing with its tail.

TIP

- Don't be fooled by the size of the bark—smaller dogs can often be more vocal than their larger relatives.

Different breeds, different barks

Barking serves as the most common means of vocal communication in dogs, and although it is often a warning, it is not necessarily aggressive in intent. The frequency of barking may vary from intermittent to frequent and can be linked with excitement (see pages 26–27) or even frustration, for example when a dog wants to come indoors, after having been out in the backyard for a while.

Individual breeds have distinctive vocalizations. Some pack hounds, such as the Bloodhound, have a very characteristic form of bark, described as "baying." This is often audible over a long distance and allows pack members to stay in close contact with each other, even in woodlands where they may be out of each other's sight. Baying also indicates that an individual has picked up a scent, and is following a trail. Nevertheless, it is not easy for humans to differentiate between most breeds and their pattern of barking. Even the tone of a bark can be misleading, simply because some small dogs, such as the Pug, can have a surprisingly deep bark, suggestive of a much larger breed. The Basenji is the only dog breed that does not bark at all.

WOLFLIKE BARKS
Sled dogs can be distinguished by their howling, which is more akin to the sounds a wolf might make, rather than other types of dogs. This reflects the close relationship and similarity in appearance between these working breeds and the Gray Wolf.

Head back When barking, a dog will raise its head in a very distinctive way, as this Shetland Sheepdog is doing. This helps to project the sound over a wider area.

Play

Young dogs have a reputation for playfulness, and they continue playing well into old age, although not as energetically. This activity helps to maintain their mental and physical health and improves their muscle tone and agility. The different ways in which dogs play is shaped early in life.

Playing styles

A dog's initial experiences establish the trends that continue throughout its life. This especially applies to the way it plays and interacts with its owner. Young puppies will instinctively chase a toy, and it is generally easy to persuade a puppy to bring the toy back as it soon realizes that you will throw it again, allowing the game to continue. Your pet's ancestry is also significant to some extent. Retrievers, for example, almost instinctively bring back toys that are thrown for them. A dog's superior sense of smell also means that it can locate toys that have fallen out of sight, for example, in a ditch or under a hedge.

Initiating play This Border Collie's posture shows that it is trying to initiate a game. It has adopted the "play bow" posture, almost lying down on its front legs with its rear in the air.

Skilled soccer players On hard surfaces, some dogs learn to use their front paws as legs, to control the movement of the ball, like a soccer player uses his or her feet when dribbling a ball.

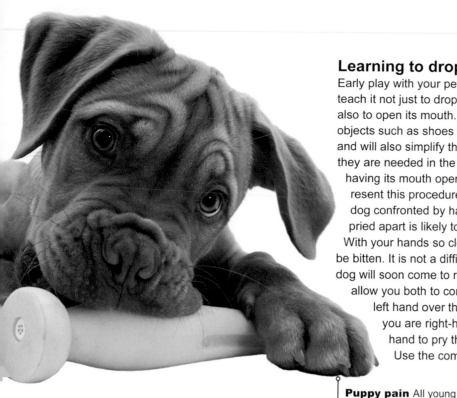

Learning to drop objects

Early play with your pet provides the opportunity to teach it not just to drop its toy when instructed, but also to open its mouth. This allows you to take away objects such as shoes that you do not want chewed and will also simplify the task of giving tablets when they are needed in the future. A dog that is used to having its mouth opened from puppyhood will not resent this procedure later in life. However, an adult dog confronted by having its jaws unexpectedly pried apart is likely to act aggressively, out of fear. With your hands so close to its jaws, you can easily be bitten. It is not a difficult lesson to teach, and your dog will soon come to realize that dropping its toy will allow you both to continue the game. Place your left hand over the top of the dog's muzzle (if you are right-handed) and use your other hand to pry the lower jaw down gently. Use the command "drop" as you do so.

Puppy pain All young dogs appreciate chew-type toys when they are teething, because they help lessen the associated irritation.

Toys for different breeds

Mastiff-type dogs, which tend to not be as athletic as many other breeds, are also less enthusiastic about chasing after a ball. Instead, they prefer toys that they can chew with their powerful jaws, or ones that can be used safely in a tug-of-war. As described above, you will need to train your pet to release the toy when instructed, as required.

SAFETY FIRST

Ensure that any toys you give to your dog are safe and appropriate and cannot harm your pet.

No teasing This English Bulldog puppy is watching the chew toy intently, sitting and waiting for it to be given to him. Avoid inadvertently teasing your pet in any way with a toy—which you can do by keeping it just out of reach—because you could cause it to become so frustrated that it tries to grab the toy aggressively.

Greetings

Dogs are very responsive to you or a family member arriving home. A dog's acute hearing, combined with an inbuilt sense of the time of day, means that it is likely to anticipate your return, especially if this happens at roughly the same time every day.

A bark of excitement

Your dog may bark if you knock against the door and when you put a key in the lock, but this will not be the kind of distinctly intimidating bark he reserves for a stranger. Instead, it will be an indication of excitement, and only repeated briefly until you enter your home and acknowledge your pet's presence.

Making eye contact Your dog will seek to gain your attention by looking intently at you as part of the greeting process.

FETCHING YOUR SLIPPERS

Dogs enjoy learning to fetch all kinds of objects; it guarantees some playful time with you. You might even be able to train your dog to fetch your slippers on your return home!

Finely tuned senses

Dogs can distinguish between the sounds of different vehicles, so your pet will soon learn to recognize when your car pulls up. This will be reinforced by the fact that your dog is likely to go out with you in the car on occasion, and so it will hear the engine sounds at closer quarters. Furthermore, its acute hearing ensures that a dog can detect your footfall as you walk to the door of your home. Each of us walks in a different way, and this gives your pet a further clue as to your distinct identity, even without hearing the sound of your voice. Although your dog might appear to be asleep when you drive up, it is likely to be alert, waiting for you to come in the door.

SAFETY FIRST

Don't let your dog out onto the street to greet you, as it might dash into the road in its enthusiasm, and end up being hit by a passing vehicle.

Touching Some dogs, such as this Labrador Retriever, will use their front paws like hands to try to touch you.

Welcoming behavior

Once you are inside, your dog is likely to greet you enthusiastically. It may jump up and weave around your legs, sniffing, especially if you have been in contact with another dog, or perhaps a cat. Rubbing itself against you also allows the dog to deposit its scent on your clothing. Finally, your pet is likely to display its excitement at seeing you again by wagging its tail enthusiastically.

Calming down again

Young dogs instinctively behave in the ways described here. The way you greet your pet will condition it to react accordingly. By stroking your pet, and acknowledging its presence, it will be reassured and quickly settle down again, perhaps even going back to sleep. However, if your dog does not get up to greet you at all, this could indicate that it is feeling unwell.

A sharp nose Your dog may be able to get information about where you have been and possibly also insight into what you have been doing, thanks to its sense of smell.

Controlling jumping up Young or small dogs, such as this Beagle puppy, are especially likely to jump up, since they cannot reach you any other way. Always respond to your dog immediately after you get in, so that it will not feel ignored. This makes it easier to discourage it from jumping up.

Visitors

The way in which a dog responds to visitors to your home will depend partly on whether the person is known to the dog, partly on the breed of dog, and partly on its training. Some dogs can become very excited by the arrival of people that they know well.

The guarding instinct

Dogs that have been bred as guard dogs will prove to be more territorial than others and will be instinctively more suspicious of visitors, especially strangers. Companion breeds, in contrast, are much more likely to be tolerant of visitors. It is important to train dogs not to react aggressively when a visitor arrives.

Two-way reaction

It is easy to simply focus on the dog's behavior when a visitor arrives but, in reality, its reaction will also be influenced by that of your guest. If the dog is approached in a nervous manner, then it is more likely to react aggressively, by growling initially, then snarling and barking ferociously as a warning. However, your dog will react to your input as well. Provided that you do not appear concerned by the presence of the visitor, your dog will soon lose interest and settle down.

Barks of excitement With the arrival of a visitor, a dog will probably utter a number of short barks in rapid succession, especially if it feels that it is being ignored. It will be looking up, waiting for a reaction.

SAFETY FIRST

A dog's claws can inflict painful scratches. Check them regularly because, if overgrown, they can become sharp at their tips.

Threatening Snarling exposes the teeth and is a direct threat.

Enthusiastic welcoming

Your dog will be able to identify and recognize regular visitors without difficulty, welcoming them excitedly. Many dogs like to jump up at this stage, with the aim of getting closer to the person's face. This is an extension of the way that dogs would naturally greet each other, by sniffing noses. Although this exuberance may seem appealing to you, it can be intimidating for the guest—especially if you have a large dog—and should not be encouraged. The dog will also probably bark in a lively, rather than a warning, manner (although this distinction may be difficult for the visitor to detect). It may also run around, possibly going away and coming back with a toy, in the hope of having a game with the visitor, too.

Territorial barking

Dogs can be aggressive when defending property. The most obvious territorial response is the way that a dog will bark if it detects the presence of a stranger. This type of barking is relatively loud and can make the dog sound as if it is larger than it actually is. The primary function is to alert you to the person's presence, and this barking should cease on your instruction. This reflects the way in which wolf packs will defend their territory, with a pack member warning the others of an incursion as soon as it is detected. Once the identity of the new arrival is clear, the dog will then modify its behavior accordingly, greeting someone it knows well, as already described.

Tail wagging A wagging tail, raised high over the back, is an easy-to-read display of your dog's enthusiasm—in dog breeds that are physically capable of this, such as this Poodle.

BARK OR BITE?

Many dogs, such as this Labrador Retriever, have a deep, often intimidating, bark. This is sufficient to cause most visitors to wait outside the gate until you call the dog back inside, rather than risk a potential confrontation. However, dogs rarely attack if someone does happen to enter unannounced, and usually just continue barking.

Standing to attention Many dogs, including Poodles, are quite adept at standing up on their hind legs, as a way of greeting visitors whom they know well. This is a means of seeking attention, to show they are not being overlooked.

Strangers

A dog's acute hearing means that it can often be aware of the approach of strangers before you hear anything at all. This is especially likely if you have a gate that has to be opened or a gravel driveway, with the dog soon learning to recognize such sounds.

The need for correct training

Puppies are usually not inclined to bark or prove especially territorial while they are young. But this changes as dogs approach sexual maturity. Particular breeds, such as the Bull Mastiff, which were developed for guarding property, will likely be suspicious toward strangers and must be properly trained to curb their aggression.

Early warning

A dog is likely to be more aware of the presence of a stranger on your property than you are, especially after dark, so if your dog starts barking intently and unexpectedly, this could be the reason. The intruder may not necessarily be a person, though—it might simply be a raccoon, for instance. While barking can give reassurance, this type of behavior does need to be controlled. It is important that the dog does not continue barking once the stranger enters your home with your permission. What you want is for your dog to settle down, having been reassured that all is well.

Big dog in a small body
Jack Russell Terriers are known for being extremely territorial and protective, and may even try to defend you if you are approached by a stranger in the street.

Temperamental Border Collies are highly intelligent but can be badly behaved and even aggressive if they are not stimulated enough.

Empty threats

Most dogs can detect when a stranger entering the home is nervous toward them, and this can encourage them to continue barking in an intimidating manner, even from elsewhere in the home. However, a dog will very rarely actually attack a stranger, although it may become involved if you yourself are assaulted by an unwanted intruder. What should happen in due course, once your dog becomes familiar with a regular visitor to the house (such as the mailman) is that it will simply bark briefly to begin with, just as it would for anyone approaching your home, and will then take no further interest.

Mailbox marauder

Dogs often do not like objects dropping through the door, such as mail or newspapers. Your pet will likely hear the approach of the delivery person and jump up and seize the items in its mouth as they fall to the ground, shaking them ferociously. It will not matter who delivered the items; the reaction will be the same.

You can fit a delivery box around your mail slot, to prevent your dog from being able to reach it, if you do not have an external mailbox. The situation is likely to be worse if the deliveries are made when you are not at home, since you cannot intervene to correct your dog's behavior. It may become increasingly aggressive and will continue barking as it defends its territory. If this is likely, keep your dog away from the area of the home where deliveries are made whenever you go out.

TIPS

- It is always sensible to let strangers know you have a dog by putting up a sign on the gate.

- Distract your dog if it starts barking at a stranger by providing a toy.

Avoiding problems

One way to prevent any problems when a stranger knocks at your door is to confine your dog in a different room while you deal with the caller. This ensures that your dog can neither start barking at the stranger, nor run out into the street. However, where a stranger is actually entering your home, a different approach will be necessary—otherwise. If you keep your dog shut up, it will become frustrated, and is likely to start scratching at the door in a bid to be let out; it will also continue barking. It is much better, assuming that your visitor is not scared of dogs, to allow your pet to meet the other person under your supervision. After this initial meeting, it will probably simply ignore both of you.

The origin
of dogs

Wolflike
behavior

Agility
training

Reading
ears

The importance
of training

The
sick dog

Reading
tails

40

Talk the Talk

How to communicate with your dog

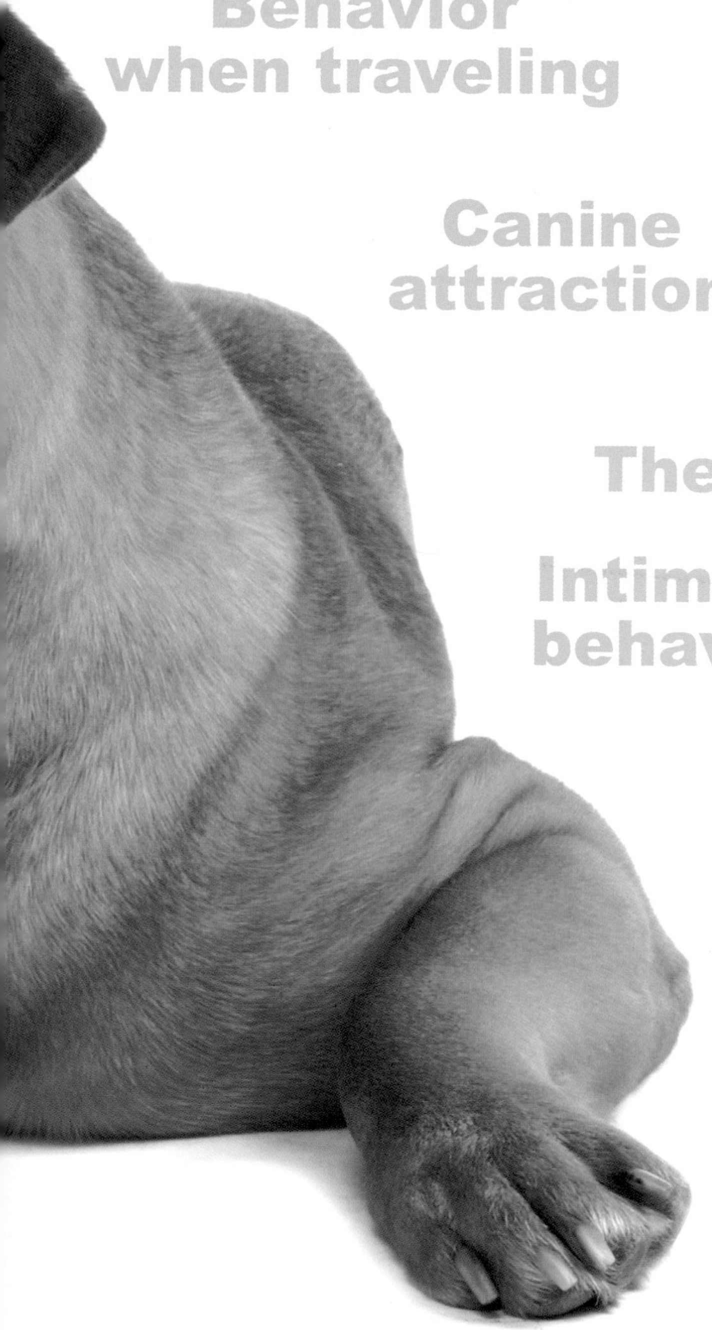

Behavior
when traveling

Breeding
behavior

Canine
attraction

The
old dog

The veterinarian

Intimate
behavior

The
tongue

Understanding
the wolf pack

Reading
the signs

The origin of dogs

It is unclear exactly how or when the domestication process of wolves began; it is unlikely to have been straightforward. Almost certainly, it took place at a number of different localities globally over the course of tens of thousands of years. All of today's domestic dog breeds are descended from the Gray Wolf.

The birth of "man's best friend"

This initial period of contact between wolves and humans is believed to have begun up to 100,000 years ago, with the domestication process that gave rise to today's dog only starting around 15,000 years ago. The transformation from wolf to dog was probably driven by changes in human society, after our ancestors started to radiate out across the globe. Communities became more settled, and agriculture began to replace the more nomadic lifestyle of the hunter-gatherer. Wolves could settle alongside people, adopting a scavenging rather than a hunting lifestyle. This fundamentally changed the relationship between people and wolves.

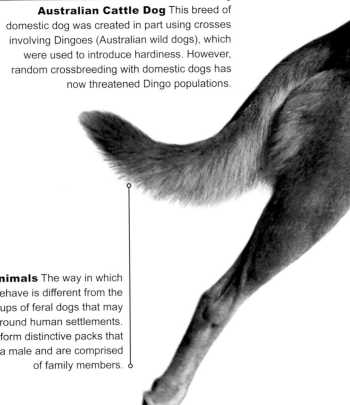

Australian Cattle Dog This breed of domestic dog was created in part using crosses involving Dingoes (Australian wild dogs), which were used to introduce hardiness. However, random crossbreeding with domestic dogs has now threatened Dingo populations.

Pack animals The way in which Dingoes behave is different from the loose groups of feral dogs that may roam around human settlements. Dingoes form distinctive packs that are led by a male and are comprised of family members.

Where domestication began

DNA analysis is now providing insights into where the process of domestication may have begun. It seems to have started in eastern Asia, and some dogs may have been taken from there across the Bering land bridge that once linked Asia to North America. There is also clear evidence that Europe became a center for domestication soon afterward. Domestic dogs can be separated from wolves on the basis of their anatomy. In particular, they lack the precaudal gland on the tail, used by the dominant male in a wolf pack to scentmark other members of the pack.

Scattered evidence

The earliest known physical remains of domestic dogs have been unearthed in Europe, although the exact date at which they were first kept is uncertain. Incomplete remains can make it difficult—a canine tooth thought to belong to a dog that existed around 31,700 years ago has been found in a Belgian cave. Strikingly, some of these finds also reveal the close bond between people and dogs. Near the German city of Düsseldorf, a dog was discovered buried alongside its master in a human grave that dated back to about 11,000 B.C.

MISSING LINK

There is no clear "missing link" between the wolf (right) and the domestic dog, although the primitive New Guinea Singing Dog, with its distinctive calls, and the better-known Australian Dingo (pictured below) may be candidates. The Dingo was domesticated around 5,000 years ago but later reverted to a free-living existence.

Shy Dingoes Dingoes hunt relatively large prey, which has brought them into serious conflict with sheep farmers in Australia, and they now avoid human contact as far as possible. In contrast, feral dogs tend to rely on scavenging for food around settlements and, although not tame, they will frequently be seen during hours of daylight, simply withdrawing if they feel threatened.

Wild but peaceful
Dingoes will fight to maintain their territory—but possibly as a legacy of their brief encounter with domestication (see box, above)—family groups of Dingoes are not as aggressive toward others of their own kind as wolves.

Understanding the wolf pack

Gray Wolves are highly social creatures, and they live in packs of varying sizes. Understanding the habits of Gray Wolves living in packs is key to understanding what makes your pet dog behave the way it does.

Hunting in packs

Gray wolves are a predatory species, with finely tuned senses that allow them to locate and hunt prey effectively. Because they live in packs, effective communication between members of the group is essential, especially when tackling potentially dangerous prey. Studies have shown that there is a direct correlation between pack size and the size of prey taken—it takes a lot of physical effort to overpower a large quarry with relative safety. Pack size is also influenced by the need to defend territory against incursions by other wolf packs.

Wolf talk Wolves rely on a combination of vocalizations and body language to communicate with each other, just like domestic dogs.

Shared responsibility As young cubs start to become independent and begin to feed on solid food, all adult members of the pack, not just their parents, will care for them.

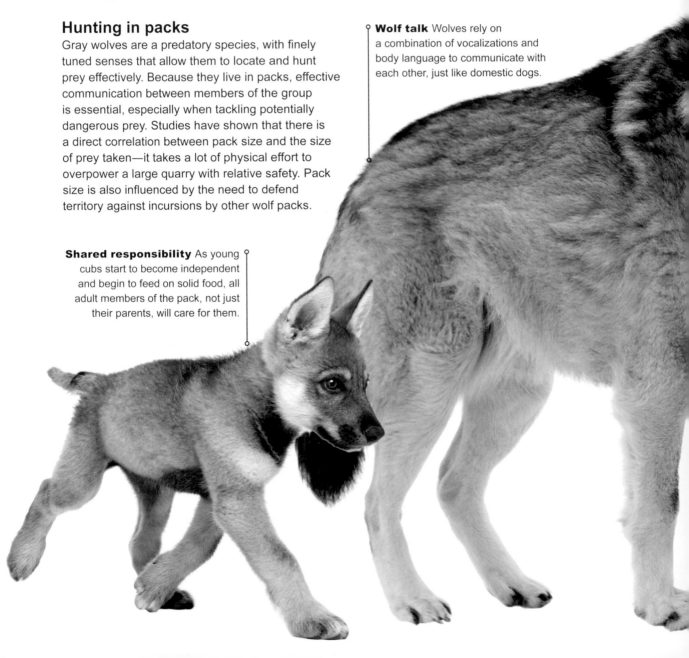

CHANGING PACK SIZE

Bigger wolf packs help ensure greater availability of food by increasing the likelihood of successful kills being made when hunting. They are also more adept at defending the resulting carcass from scavengers. If food does become short, however, pack numbers will fall, with weaker individuals being driven out.

Geographical variations The largest wolf packs can be found in northern parts of North America, where caribou are the typical prey. Here, packs of nine or more individuals are common, but in the Middle East, where wolves hunt smaller quarry, they often live individually or in pairs.

Fitting in Young wolves are much more likely than older ones to be accepted by a new pack.

Pack hierarchy

Relationships within the wolf pack are important, binding pack members together. The pack is essentially a family group led by a dominant pair of wolves, with pack members recognizing each other by sight and scent. Within a pack, members seek to avoid conflict, and maintain a strict hierarchy; it is usual for only the dominant pair to breed. Packs are usually aggressive toward solitary adult wolves that enter their territory and will fight to repel any incursions by neighboring packs, defending their hunting domain.

Recognition and acceptance

Bonds between packs can also extend over a surprising distance. In cases where a pack member has moved successfully into a new pack, other individuals from the original pack are more likely to be accepted into the new pack in the future. This has been confirmed by DNA testing, which revealed that packs spread over a large area can be related to each other. This suggests that scent recognition is very important among wolves. This reliance on scent, in terms of recognizing individuals, is also very apparent in the domestic dog.

Wolflike behavior

Many of the behaviors seen in domestic dogs today are also evident in wolves—although dogs have also developed some that are unique, typically relating to their relationship with people. The way in which such behaviors evolve has been revealed in part by the breeding of hybrid "wolf-dogs."

Vocalization Dogs and wolves do have some similar vocalization patterns, but they also differ in a number of respects. Dogs bark far more readily than wolves, having been encouraged to do so for a variety of reasons, frequently linked to their working roles.

Working behavior Dogs have developed different patterns of behavior from wolves, and these vary greatly across the breeds. The behavior of a particular breed is likely to be a reflection of its working ancestry.

Appearance range Some dogs are much farther removed from wolves in their appearance than others, and are less likely to exhibit lupine (wolflike) behavior. This dog is not very wolflike in appearance at all.

Wolf-dog hybrids

A chance to study the differences in behavior between wolves and their domestic relatives arose as the result of one man's concerns about the weaknesses of domestic dogs—specifically the German Shepherd's susceptibility to distemper (a common illness afflicting domestic dogs that can now be prevented by vaccination). Dutchman Leendert Saarloos mated a male German Shepherd with a female Eurasian Wolf for his study but initially ended up with an unexpected result: the offspring died from distemper. Undeterred by this setback, however, Saarloos persevered and was finally rewarded with a litter of healthy hybrid offspring. This provided a unique opportunity to observe exactly what aspects of wolf behavior could be seen in the early domesticated dogs.

A wolflike dog

Saarloos' wolf-dog hybrids proved to be far more wary than domestic dogs and tended to remain together in a pack. If one of the youngsters was separated from its companions, it became decidedly nervous and refused to settle down, instead roaming around and looking for them. The animals were not aggressive, and tended to communicate more by howling than by barking. Another area where a marked difference between wolves and dogs had previously been observed was in their reaction to training; wolves were far more resistant to this concept than domestic dogs. As the breeding program progressed, though, the emerging hybrid breed became more doglike in its attributes. Saarloos continued his breeding program right up until his death in 1969, establishing a recognizable type for these dogs, which has seen them accepted by the Dutch Kennel Club for show purposes. But even now, the Saarlooswolfhond—as the breed is known—will not thrive if kept individually; owners generally have two or more animals to preserve the feel of a pack.

The Czech approach

A similar breeding program involving Gray Wolves and German Shepherd dogs began in 1955, in what was then Czechoslovakia. This resulted in a breed that differs in temperament from the Saarlooswolfhond. The Czechoslovakian Vlčák (see box, above right) is very similar to a wolf in appearance but lacks the shyness associated with Saarloos' dogs.

A WORKING DOG

Ease of movement and considerable stamina are features of the Czechoslovakian Vlčák, which closely resembles the Gray Wolf (above). Socialization from an early age is vital, in terms of ensuring a well-adjusted adult dog, and training is not too difficult, although a breed-specific approach is recommended, relying on motivation rather than repetition. These dogs have been used successfully in Italy for search and rescue purposes (see page 156 for more about search and rescue dogs).

Head size The head is smaller in domestic dogs than in wolves, as shown here, and this is a feature that usually helps distinguish wolf-dogs from pure wolves when seen together.

Reading the signs

With some types of dogs, it is easier to obtain insights into their behavior from their general demeanor than others. Understanding their body language and behavior is especially important when you are out walking with your own pet, as it can help you avoid confrontation with other dogs.

General demeanor

Some dogs, such as Retrievers, look relaxed and confident when they are trotting along, showing no signs of nervousness or aggression. Dogs that are naturally social, such as Beagles and similar scenthounds, are usually well disposed toward other dogs. However, certain scenthound individuals may be unsure of themselves when meeting strangers for the first time.

Dogs of all types that have been mistreated in the past can be less predictable in their behavior, and you should err on the side of caution in order to prevent your dog from running off if it is scared or becoming aggressive if cornered. Ensure that your dog is responsive to your commands, so that you can call it back to your side if necessary.

Relaxed Cocker Spaniels are a breed developed to work with humans and tend to have a relaxed demeanor.

Slightly unsure This Chinese Crested Dog looks slightly unsure of itself. Although its ears are held forward and kept upright, its tail is tucked back under its body.

Socialization

One way to help prevent a dog from behaving in an inappropriate manner is to arrange to take your pet to puppy socialization classes. These are not training sessions; they simply allow the dogs to mix at an early stage, so there is less likelihood of conflict when they grow older. By learning to play with each other from puppyhood, the theory is that dogs should become more tolerant. Canine aggression in many cases is caused by fear.

The importance of ears This dog is able to communicate its moods and intentions using its expressive, mobile ears (see pages 50–51). This ability will allow it to avoid conflict in certain situations. Some dog breeds have their ears cropped (although this practice is decreasing in most places) to make their ears stand erect. This takes away a method of communication and may incite acts of aggression between dogs as a result.

Anticipating trouble

Some breeds are less well disposed to others of their species, which is where observation on your part becomes very important. Do not automatically assume that all Staffordshire Bull Terriers are aggressive toward other dogs because of their dog-fighting ancestry. However, you should be aware that if you own one of these dogs, and you meet a fellow dog-owner coming toward you on a narrow path, there is greater potential for conflict between the dogs than if they were in a large field where you could call your pet back to you and walk in a different direction.

Friend or foe?

Relative size is not an entirely reliable indicator of how dogs will react to each other; some small breeds—even the Chihuahua, which is the smallest of all—can be quite feisty on occasions. Dogs are like people, in that they meet some individuals that they apparently like and get along with, chasing around excitedly when off the leash, while others cause them to raise their hackles and adopt an aggressive pose. It is often impossible to predict their reaction with any certainty, so watch carefully for any signs of trouble.

TIP

• The presence of a bitch in heat will cause male dogs to behave more aggressively toward each other.

Frown of concentration Pugs have a tightly curled tail, so they rely primarily on the position of their ears to indicate their mood. When concentrating, with their ears pulled forward, they may (misleadingly) appear worried as the loose skin on the forehead becomes more wrinkled.

A few guidelines

There are some general guidelines about how different dogs will react to one another. Unneutered male dogs are most likely to be aggressive, and there is no doubt that dogs do remember each other if you walk in the same area regularly. On the other hand, dogs can form friendships and be playful, with one individual bounding up to another and dropping down on its front legs in a play bow (see page 83). Age has a bearing, too, with such playful behavior most common in younger dogs.

Reading ears

For visual communication, dogs use their ears to indicate their moods and reactions in particular situations, although the significance of this type of communication varies according to the breed. The shape of the ears, and their relative flexibility, are both significant factors.

Different ear styles

The ears of dogs differ significantly in appearance between breeds. Spitz-type dogs, which are closest to the Gray Wolf in appearance, have conspicuous, erect ears that are not especially mobile. Their ears are quite thick and well protected against the cold of the northern areas where such breeds were developed.

At the other extreme are some of the herding breeds, such as the Hungarian Komondor, which has a matted coat that obscures its ears.

Ears that are erect can enable dogs to pinpoint the source of sounds more easily, and it is no coincidence that they are seen mainly in breeds that work primarily in open countryside, as in the case of members of the Spitz group, which have frequently served as sled dogs. Those that work in undergrowth, such as most sporting hounds, have long ears that hang down. These serve to protect their sensitive ear canals from being injured by sharp, protruding pieces of vegetation that may be encountered when running through this type of terrain.

Relaxed pose This dog's ears are upright, as is typical of Spitz-type breeds. However, you can tell it is relaxed as the skin is not drawn back taut behind the eyes.

No control Young puppies, such as these Corgis, may not be able to use their ears effectively for communication, as they simply hang down at first.

Guilty Listening intently, and with its rather worried look, this puppy is clearly concerned that it has misbehaved.

Barometers of mood

One aspect of canine body language has even entered our own language. The description of "hangdog" is well known, and is used to describe a person who appears downcast and guilty. This phrase is a direct reflection of the way that a dog that has misbehaved will react when it is scolded—it will allow its ears to hang down lower than usual. The same applies to the position of its tail, which also droops. In contrast, a happy, attentive dog will have its ears raised slightly, looking intently in the direction of whatever might have attracted its attention. Its tail is also likely to be held upright.

Obstructing communication

Ear cropping is a surgical procedure that is now outlawed in many countries for being cruel and unnecessary. The procedure entails removing some of the cartilage from each ear so that the ears are permanently raised in a vertical position. This is sometimes carried out in large breeds such as the Great Dane, with the intention of making the dog look more ferocious. However, by fixing the ears in this position, it becomes impossible for the dog to use its ears to communicate effectively. Dogs that are not able to communicate as effectively as they normally would are more likely to become involved in fights. This, in turn, tends to reinforce the aggressive link associated with the practice of ear cropping.

Alert and confident
The Beagle is a breed that has expressive ears. Here, the ears are drawn forward, the head is slightly tilted to the side, and the eyes are focused, indicating alertness.

Manipulation Chihuahuas, like this long-coated example, have enormous, expressive ears. They can be a bit manipulative, charming their owners into doing things they don't want to do.

Reading tails

Dogs use their tails to communicate their moods, frequently in conjunction with the movement of their ears (see pages 50–51). The emphasis on the use of the tail for communication varies, depending on the breed concerned. Dogs can communicate a wide range of behaviors with their tails, from excitement to aggression.

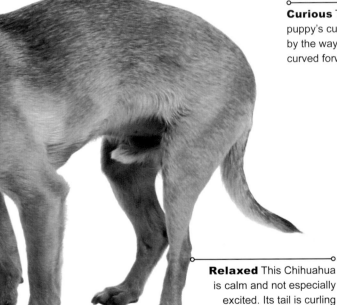

Curious This Chihuahua puppy's curiosity is shown by the way its tail is curved forward.

Relaxed This Chihuahua is calm and not especially excited. Its tail is curling down gently toward its tip, held away from its body.

SAFETY FIRST

Hunting dogs sometimes suffer from muscular damage to the tail, known as "limber tail." With a few weeks rest, the tail should recover.

Tail talk

Some dogs are better equipped to communicate with their tails than others. Breeds such as herding dogs tend not to rely on their tails to any significant extent, whereas many toy breeds, such as the Chihuahuas shown on these pages, use their tails as a very important means of communicating with their owners. The tail provides an instant way of indicating their mood, which can then be responded to.

Reading the signs

A raised tail signifies that a dog is alert and paying attention to what is happening in its environment. Such behavior can soon lead to a more engaged response, with the dog wagging its tail enthusiastically from side to side. This signifies excitement, with dogs usually greeting their owners in this way if they have been separated for any length of time. Should the tail be extended in a more horizontal position, this can be a sign of uncertainty, while a tail that is tucked down between the hind legs is typically seen in a nervous or chastened individual. Prominent tails can run the risk of being badly injured, though, in the case of sporting dogs, and this is why the tails of dogs kept entirely for field work are still sometimes docked in countries that otherwise ban this practice.

Tail variations

Just as with the ears, there is considerable variation in tail shape, size, and flexibility, which accounts for the varying emphasis placed on the tail in canine communication between different breeds. One of the characteristics of the Spitz group of breeds, for example, is the way that their tails curl down over the back and forward to one side. A few breeds, especially members of the herding group, may be born with tails that are much shorter than normal, or even absent; these individuals are known as "bobtails."

Breeds with long coats have longer fur on their tails as well, so their tails are heavier and less flexible when it comes to communication. Many smooth-coated hounds, such as the Bloodhound, have tails that allow pack members to spot them easily when they are pursuing their quarry through undergrowth. It is for this reason that they tend to display them held high over their backs.

Tail stretch This Chihuahua has just woken up and is stretching its tail as well as its body. It may extend the tail horizontally at first, before wagging it from side to side and then keeping it raised, while waiting to see what is happening. A range of muscles are responsible for controlling the position of the tail and its movements.

Holding steady Having exercised its tail muscles, the Chihuahua keeps its tail upright, while it continues stretching. If it suffers any injury to its tail, this can cause paralysis of the muscles, which will restrict its ability to move its tail in this way.

Possible concern This Chihuahua is not sure of what is happening on its left-hand side. This is reflected by the way that the ear on this side of the head is drawn back, while its tail is kept low and directed to the right. A narrowing series of bones runs along the tail to support the muscles and nerves that control its movements.

The tongue

A dog's muscular tongue is an essential part of its anatomy. It is used for functional purposes, such as grooming, tasting, and cooling down, and for communication both with humans and other dogs.

Tongue facts

A dog's tongue is generally pink, with two notable exceptions: the Shar-Pei (see page 69) and the Chow Chow, both Chinese breeds. These both have dark, bluish tongues, a scarce characteristic among over 400 recognized dog breeds.

Dogs can extend their tongues to lick the fur at the sides of their mouths. If they have the remains of a meal sticking to the fur there, they can wipe it away, and they may also be joined in this task by other dogs! They also use their tongues to groom their coats over a wider area, sometimes nibbling at the skin, as well as licking the fur. This can help remove stains and mud, as well as helping to keep the dog's body temperature down in hot weather.

Dogs do not have sweat glands all over their bodies—these are confined to the area between the toes and the soles of the feet. The evaporation of saliva from the tongue's surface is what helps them regulate their body temperature.

A dog relies on the muscular nature of its tongue to create a kind of "ladle" when it drinks, allowing it to lap up water efficiently. The tongue also helps position food for swallowing, especially important when you bear in mind that dogs tend to gulp their food down, rather than chewing it into small pieces first.

Potential danger The tongue has a large blood supply, so any injury to it can result in profuse bleeding. An opened can, especially the lid, is a particular danger, because if your dog licks it, it could easily cut its tongue.

Strong and flexible
A dog's tongue is both very muscular and flexible. It can be extended from the mouth and directed around the lips and may even reach up to the nose, as shown here.

Puppy care

Mothers with newborn puppies use their tongues to lick their young quite vigorously after suckling. This encourages newborn offspring to relieve themselves, until such a time that they develop more effective bowel and bladder control.

Licking as a health indicator

Dogs also use their tongues to relieve irritation on their bodies. They may suddenly start licking their paws repeatedly in late summer, after being out walking in the countryside—this is a classic sign of infestation by the larval form of the harvest mite (*Trombicula autumnalis*). Be careful if you suspect this, because the irritation from these parasites can be so intense that your dog may snap at you if you try to examine the affected area.

Dogs will also lick any actual wounds on their body, with the aim of restricting blood loss and guarding against infection. Repeated licking of the lower leg will result in a bald area called a "lick granuloma." This often indicates a psychological illness, and is especially common in larger dogs regularly left alone for long periods.

Be observant Frequent, repeated licking in one area may be indicative of an underlying health problem. This Boxer is licking repeatedly at its paw, which could suggest a mite infestation.

TIP

• *Continual licking of one part of the body may be linked to an underactive thyroid gland. If you suspect this, get your dog checked by the veterinarian.*

More reasons for licking

A dog may lick around the lips of another dog as a sign of submission. This action has its origins in puppyhood, when a puppy will lick around the sides of its mother's mouth in the hope of encouraging her to regurgitate food (see page 80). This could explain why your dog will try to lick your face. In addition, young dogs like to lick objects—this is probably partly out of curiosity, as a way of investigating texture.

FACE LICKING

When a dog meets another dog that it knows well, the two will often sniff each other initially, before licking each other's faces. Dogs, and especially young dogs, also try to do this as a greeting to their owner. This is why your dog may sometimes leap up when you bend down or jump onto your lap when you sit down, and begin to lick your face. It is a friendly greeting, but clearly not behavior to encourage on the grounds of hygiene. If your dog is wearing a collar, it will be much easier to persuade it to desist, as you can control it more easily. Otherwise, you will simply need to push it gently away, instructing it to sit.

Canine attraction

Just as with people, there is no obvious reason why some dogs seem to like each other. But once they have formed a bond, this is likely to be a long-lasting friendship, with the dogs recognizing each other and remaining friendly, even if they are then separated for long periods.

Unsure This older Labrador Retriever puppy is not quite sure about the Whippet Lurcher cross puppy, shown not just by his suspicious gaze, but also by the way in which the ears are drawn back and slightly raised.

Comfortable together Dogs that are related, such as these Border Collies, or that live in the same household, are likely to get along well.

Living together

Where there are family ties between dogs, such as mother and daughter, or two siblings that have grown up together, they will almost certainly get along well throughout their lives. Where such dogs are living together, there is already an established order, and this will not be challenged. However, most puppies will bond well even when from different litters, and obtaining two at the same time should improve the chances of a close relationship. They may occasionally have a disagreement, but this tends to be over food, or perhaps a toy, and is unlikely to result in serious conflict. You can avoid problems of this type by feeding them separately.

Expressing a close bond

After a period apart, closely bonded dogs should be pleased to see each other again, sniffing each other and often barking excitedly by way of a greeting. However, if one of your dogs has a tendency to be aggressive, reintroduce them with care, and supervise them for the first few minutes. Their play could become boisterous if the dogs roll over and wrestle with each other. If the hackles along the back are not raised, you can assume the encounter is a friendly one. Both dogs may take turns running after each other, even though it is likely that one will be dominant.

Casual acquaintances

Dogs that do not live together but meet regularly, perhaps out on a walk, may also strike up a friendly relationship. As soon as one spots the other, it is likely to run forward, wagging its tail. The dogs will sniff each other and circle around, before chasing off after one another, probably in a circle, looping around you and the other dog's owner. There is no evidence that dogs will be more social with members of their own breed. In fact, dogs of totally different types, such as a Pug and a Greyhound, can strike up a relationship, although their physique may impact the way they play together.

Building a relationship

When you need to be sure that dogs will get along, there are some steps you can take to increase the likelihood of this outcome. Most importantly, do not simply bring one dog home and expect the established dog to accept it immediately, as this will almost certainly lead to conflict, with the newcomer encroaching on the territory of the existing dog. This will take time and patience. It will be much better to allow the dogs to meet on neutral territory, such as a park, on several occasions first, so they can get to know each other before taking them back home together. Strange as it may seem, you should not give reassurance to the newcomer. You need to emphasize from the outset that the established dog here is in charge, so as not to undermine its position. Make a fuss over the established dog first. As with young puppies, avoid potential conflict at mealtimes by feeding the dogs separately.

Getting along Two friendly dogs will often launch into a game; this particular individual is play bowing to another dog as a clear invitation to play.

Intimate behavior

Dogs develop unique ways of communicating with those in their immediate circle—canine or human. This is linked in part to the routine that they followed while growing up, which will have helped them determine how best to attract attention (see pages 22–23). They rely largely on body language for these purposes.

Getting what it wants

At close quarters, eye contact between dog and owner is significant. In order to attract your attention, your dog might place its head on your leg if you are sitting down or gently place its paw there, while looking at you all the time. This should be sufficient to get you to make a fuss over your pet—once you start moving, it will run off excitedly, in anticipation of a walk or its food. If you fail to react as anticipated, however, then your dog will return to your side and repeat this routine.

For your eyes only

In order to get back onto its feet from lying on its back, a dog would need to roll over first to get onto its side before regaining its footing. It is the time it would take to reach a defensive stance that makes this a trusting posture, especially because the vulnerable underside of the neck is exposed when the dog is in this position. Dogs may also switch to lying in this position when asleep, if they are warm and relaxed. It allows the dog to cool down by exposing its underparts where there is less fur present, so it can lose heat more easily.

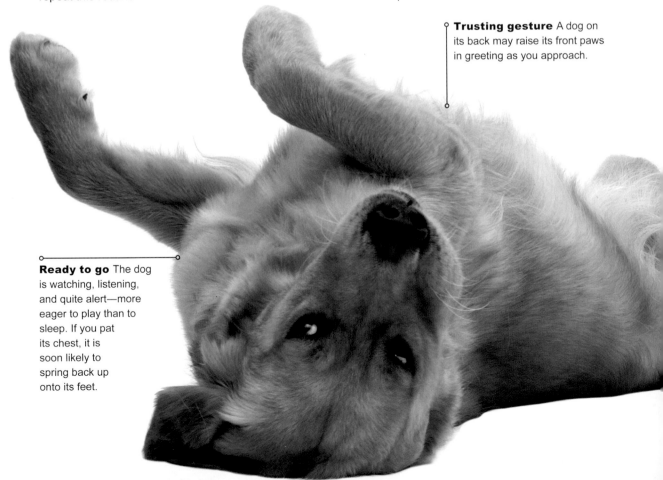

Trusting gesture A dog on its back may raise its front paws in greeting as you approach.

Ready to go The dog is watching, listening, and quite alert—more eager to play than to sleep. If you pat its chest, it is soon likely to spring back up onto its feet.

Best of friends Both of these dogs are very relaxed meeting each other, a sign that they know each other well and are renewing their acquaintance. Dogs that have been apart for a time will go through a ritual of sniffing different areas of the other dog's body when they are reunited.

Top dog In canine terms, staring is a key indicator of dominance, with the more submissive individual breaking off its gaze first.

Reasons for rolling

A dog may roll on its back for several reasons. If it is on the ground, then this is often an indication that it would like to play. It may start to paw at you with its front legs and then leap up, knowing it has your attention, and running off before returning with a toy. Should your dog be lying on a sofa next to you, however, this is simply an indication that it wants you to make a fuss over it and stroke its chest and belly. A dog will typically roll over in this way when it is warm after having been curled up. Afterward, it may then end up turning over onto its side rather than lying on its back, which is not a particularly comfortable posture for a dog to adopt for any length of time. Dogs may also roll around like this when playing with each other, as part of an exuberant game, with one dog on its back. They will use their legs to wrestle with each other. This is a sign of two dogs that know each other well, rather than a more aggressive encounter, where both dogs will be eager to stay on their feet.

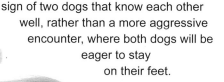

SAFETY FIRST

When two dogs meet, watch for signs that tell you how they feel about each other. For information on aggression, see pages 112–113.

LIMBERING UP

Out in a yard, a dog will roll on its back in this way to stretch itself, rather like us flexing our back or stretching when we stand up. The power in the dog's back will be quite apparent in this instance, as it will be able to move some distance by wriggling along. Just be aware, though, that a dog may also roll in this way to cover itself in the dung of other animals, ranging from foxes to cattle, thereby acquiring that pungent odor itself.

Breeding behavior

Most female dogs have two seasons of reproductive activity, referred to as "heat," each year. There are a few exceptions, however—the primitive African hunting dog, known as the Basenji, has just one, in common with the wolf. Once they are sexually mature, bitches will continue to come into heat throughout their lives.

Start of the process

The behavior of a bitch will change as she comes into heat. She will become noticeably restless, and although male dogs will be attracted to her, she will reject any attempts to mate at this stage, although they may play together. This period lasts on average for about nine days, although it can be anything from two to 27 days. Subsequently, however, during the estrus phase of the bitch's cycle, evident from a bloody vaginal discharge which can gradually become straw-colored, mating will occur. This is the stage at which ovulation occurs; the eggs are released from the ovary and are ready to be fertilized. They start developing in the uterus before implanting in the uterine wall, where each fetus develops a separate placental connection to the mother.

A PLACE TO GIVE BIRTH

Bitches will seek out a secluded spot in the home where they can give birth, just as a wild dog will retreat to a cave or a den where its young will be hidden. Provide the whelping box a week before the puppies are due, so the bitch can become accustomed to it. Otherwise, she may give birth elsewhere.

Powerful pheromones

Female dogs in estrus produce chemical messengers called "pheromones," which are carried on air currents. Although undetectable to us, these are very effective at alerting male dogs throughout the neighborhood that there is a bitch in heat. Avoid taking her out for a walk at this stage, and supervise her in the backyard, too. She will be eager to escape and run off in the hope of finding a partner. A bitch may mate with several male dogs in rapid succession, so puppies in the same litter often have different fathers.

TIP

- *Bitches will continue to have seasons throughout their lives, unless they have been spayed.*

Sign of pregnancy The bitch's mammary glands will become enlarged and pinker toward the end of her pregnancy.

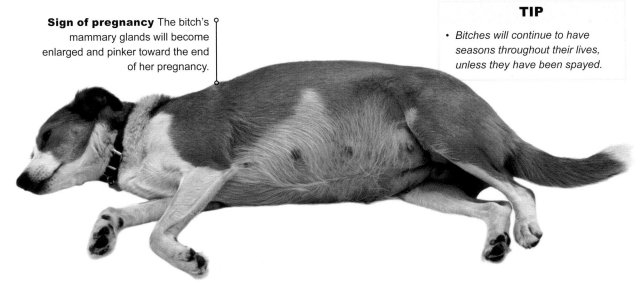

Pregnancy and birth

If the bitch becomes pregnant during her season, it will be another 63 days on average before her puppies are born. As the pregnancy nears its end, she will be eager to find a quiet area where she can give birth without disturbance (see box, opposite). In the initial stages of labor, she will show signs of distress, lose her appetite, and may sometimes howl because of the contractions. Such symptoms are more likely to be severe in bitches whelping for the first time. A fall in her body temperature is one of the most reliable indicators that the appearance of the puppies is imminent, along with a vulval discharge. About a day later, straining becomes apparent and the puppies are born, with a typical gap of about 30 minutes between each one. Occasionally, there can be problems, as puppies can become stuck, and may have to be born by Caesarean section.

Early days

The afterbirths—the placentas that nourished each puppy through its gestation period—should be ejected after each birth. The bitch is likely to eat these, which may seem alarming but is quite normal behavior. Wild dogs behave in a similar way, because the presence of the afterbirths is likely to attract potential predators. Once her litter is complete, the bitch will lie down, giving her offspring their first opportunity to suckle. This is very important, because it will provide the puppies with antibodies, helping protect them from infections until their own immune systems are functioning fully. These antibodies are only present in the bitch's milk for the first two days, during which time they can be absorbed by the puppy's body. Speak with your vet about early deworming, because puppies can be infected with these parasites even before birth.

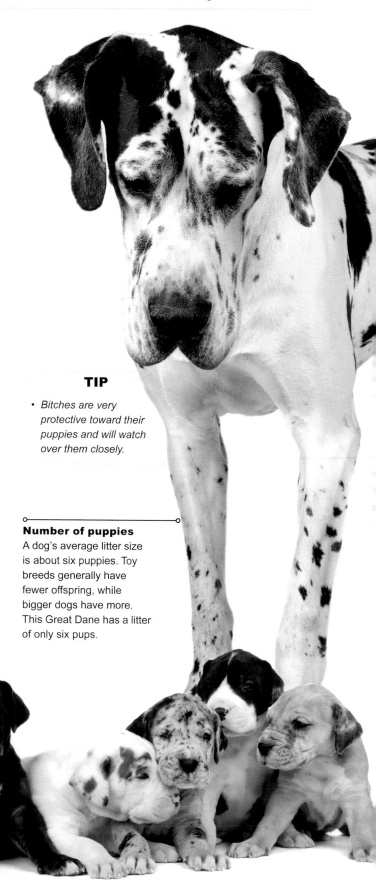

TIP

- *Bitches are very protective toward their puppies and will watch over them closely.*

Number of puppies
A dog's average litter size is about six puppies. Toy breeds generally have fewer offspring, while bigger dogs have more. This Great Dane has a litter of only six pups.

The sick dog

You will almost instinctively know when your dog is sick, even if it is not showing obvious signs, such as vomiting. The subtle changes in a dog's behavior will help alert you to the problem, even though the underlying reason may be unclear.

Common indicators

The causes of ill health in dogs are various, as are the symptoms, but there are usually some general behavioral signs that show up, regardless of the cause. Your dog is likely to be less lively and responsive and not as eager to get up and eat or go for a walk as usual. If it is in pain for any reason, it may growl unexpectedly when you touch it, and if you keep on, you may even be bitten.

Handling a sick dog

Some dogs, especially the toy breeds, may act as if they are not feeling well, because they have learned from past experience that this is a way of getting more attention from their owners. In the majority of cases, though, the dog will be genuinely sick and you will need to take your pet to the veterinarian without delay. Be careful when moving a dog that is in pain, though, as it may become aggressive. Take particular care when picking up a sick dog, as you could easily be bitten. The safest way is to fit your pet with a suitable muzzle before attempting this.

TIP

• *Consider insuring your pet to protect you from unexpected veterinary costs.*

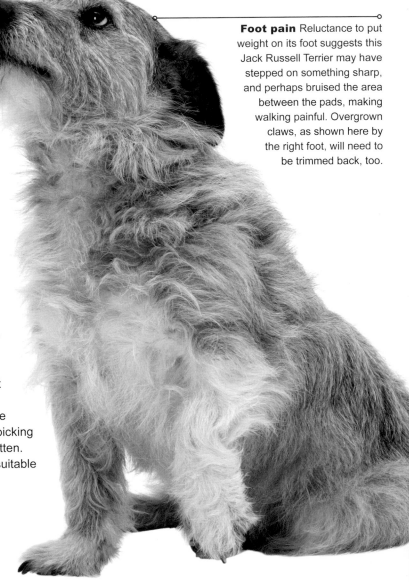

Foot pain Reluctance to put weight on its foot suggests this Jack Russell Terrier may have stepped on something sharp, and perhaps bruised the area between the pads, making walking painful. Overgrown claws, as shown here by the right foot, will need to be trimmed back, too.

Watch for body language

Your dog's body language will tell you that it is under the weather, and it may be possible to determine which part of the body is affected, too. Most dogs that are ill will look rather stressed and fearful, with their ears drawn back and their tail held low, sometimes with a hunched-over appearance when they move. This may indicate the possibility of intestinal pain. It could be a sign of a generalized infection, with the dog's body temperature being raised. Alternatively, it may be that your dog has swallowed a "foreign body." Such behavior is quite common in young dogs, which may ingest a wide variety of objects.

Examples of injuries

The dog pawing and nibbling intently at its body is a sign of irritation, and this is often seen with parasites. A so-called "flea bite allergy" (see page 14) may be the underlying cause; just a single bite can trigger this type of reaction. In cases where the dog is having difficulty moving, shown by limping, the problem may reside in the limbs, but equally, there might be a back injury. Due to their long bodies, Dachshunds are especially susceptible to slipped disks, and they should never be encouraged to jump up onto a chair or go upstairs, as these activities increase the risk of this happening. Always treat your dog with great care if it loses the use of its legs, carrying it in a horizontal position to avoid worsening the problem; remember that it will be distressed, so act accordingly.

Nursing your pet back to health

There are plenty of ways in which you can help your pet recover, by the general care that you provide, alongside the prescribed treatment. Dogs respond well to reassurance, so speaking with your pet in a soft voice and stroking him will help. When a dog is not eating well, you can improve your pet's appetite by cooking fresh food, such as chicken, and offering it warm (not hot!) rather than cold. Offering your pet food by hand may encourage it to start eating again, if it is reluctant to do so. Be sure that your dog can drink easily by providing a shallow water bowl, and make sure it can get outside to relieve itself, as it will be reluctant to soil in the home, and this could otherwise lead to constipation.

Reassurance Your dog will need plenty of reassurance, whatever its condition. Its body language clearly shows that this dog is fearful.

Rehabilitation With the right treatment, you should notice a fairly rapid improvement in your pet's health. Today, rehabilitation from injuries may include courses of hydrotherapy or chiropractic manipulation, alongside standard veterinary care.

The veterinarian

Many dogs dislike going to visit the veterinarian. Once they realize where they are, they will likely try to pull away, or simply sit down. This behavior will be related to bad memories of previous visits; it is possible to prevent dogs from developing this fear.

Positive experiences

Avoiding the fear is much easier to accomplish in the case of puppies than older dogs, whose view of the world is already formed. There are now more opportunities for puppies to develop positive memories about trips to the veterinarian than in the past, as increasing numbers of veterinary clinics offer socialization classes for puppies, where they can simply come and play together, or "well puppy" sessions, where owners can obtain advice and have their pet checked over at the same time.

The start of problems

There will obviously be times when your dog does need actual veterinary treatment, even if it is just a routine vaccination. Your pet will pick up on your mood, and if you are nervous, this could cause your puppy to become fearful and start acting up, especially if it has been scared by other dogs while in the waiting room.

Hard to understand Fixing this Collie's fractured leg will ultimately bring it relief, but it will not show any gratitude because it will not understand. Instead, it is more likely to try to gnaw off the dressing.

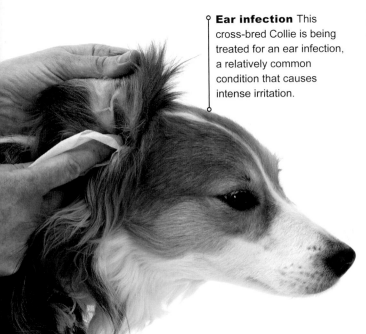

Ear infection This cross-bred Collie is being treated for an ear infection, a relatively common condition that causes intense irritation.

Possible problems

Young puppies tend to be quite positive by nature, and your veterinarian will be eager to build on this attitude for the future. In most cases, puppies feel nothing when they are given a vaccination in the loose skin at the back of the neck, nor indeed when they are microchipped, which is vital for identification purposes. Problems are more likely to arise, however, if your dog is already in pain and needs to restrained in order to be examined. Your veterinarian may recommend a temporary muzzle. This will be safer for everyone, although depending on your dog's condition, it may need to be sedated as well.

Sedation and anesthesia

Unfortunately, dogs usually do not appreciate when they are being helped, and this may cause problems, both during treatment and throughout the recovery phase. However, there are now very effective means of sedation and anesthesia for dogs, as well as pain relief, so this will not only make the whole process less stressful for the dog, but it should also mean that treatment can be given more effectively, without the dog struggling and attempting to bite and break free. Dogs are usually back on their feet very rapidly, even after major surgery.

Pain-free procedure
This Bulldog puppy is quite unperturbed by the fact that it is being microchipped. The microchip contains a unique code that identifies the dog. It should remain in place and function throughout the dog's life (see page 131).

TIP

• *Be sure to follow instructions for giving tablets very carefully. You may be able to disguise tablets for your dog in its food.*

Keeping bandages in place
Trying to keep bandages on a dog can be difficult. Bandages on the head can be protected using a plastic "halo" to keep the dog from scratching them off.

Recovery from surgery

Even if a dog needs to be hospitalized for a while, don't worry—it will not forget you or display any lingering resentment for having been left at the veterinary clinic. Dogs live very much for the moment, and your pet's enthusiasm will be directed toward seeing you again and then exploring familiar surroundings when you get home together. However excited it is, your dog should not be encouraged to jump up and run around soon after surgery, though, because of its sutures.

The old dog

The age at which dogs are considered "old" varies because of the differences in their life spans, which are related to their size. A giant breed such as a Great Dane could be considered old by the age of six, whereas a small terrier may not be regarded as old for a further three years.

TIP

- *Puppies can give a new lease on life to an older dog, but be sure that the puppy does not injure the older dog when they play.*

New tricks Puppies will learn from older dogs, and so having a well-trained older dog around may make it easier to train a puppy.

Long claws This Jack Russell Terrier has long claws due to walking less with advancing age.

Misleading sign

The most obvious sign of aging is often assumed to be the graying of the fur around a dog's muzzle, which is particularly evident in black dogs; however, this may be apparent in dogs that are only two or three years old. This loss of pigmentation is very localized in any case, and is not seen elsewhere on the body.

SAFETY FIRST

Regular health checks two or three times a year are recommended for older dogs to address any underlying medical problems.

Weight gain

As a dog grows older, it will generally exercise less, but will continue to eat the same amount of food. As a result, it will start to put on weight. This, in turn, will put more stress and strain on its joints, reducing its level of activity still further and marking the start of a downward spiral. An obese dog will be vulnerable to a number of associated health problems, including a greater risk of heart disease and diabetes mellitus. It is a good idea to switch an older dog to a "senior" diet, which is more suited to its needs and contains fewer calories, and to monitor its weight. Don't forget to cut back on tidbits as well, which can be a significant cause of weight gain.

Gradual process

Aging will affect a dog's behavior gradually. An older dog will be less mobile and will not want to walk as far as before. This makes it more likely that the claws will become overgrown and need trimming. Signs of lameness affecting the hips may be apparent first thing in the morning or after a walk, when movement seems painful. The eyes may become cloudy as cataracts form, but usually, a dog's ability to find its way around will not be seriously impaired. Its hearing may decline with age. In the case of breeds such as the Pug, characterized by their flat noses, they are likely to breathe and snore louder. There is little that can be done to ease this, although it may be worth asking your veterinarian to check for nasal tumors, a symptom of which is recurrent nosebleeds.

Hot and bothered This Labrador Retriever has become significantly overweight as it has grown older, and this makes it more uncomfortable in warm surroundings, causing it to pant more frequently.

Hidden age
This elderly Giant Schnauzer has graying hair around the jaws—a sign of old age. Many dogs show few outward signs of aging and remain active well into old age.

Mental changes

It can be much harder than you might think to distinguish physical and mental deterioration in the case of an older dog. The reduction in its hearing ability, for example, may cause it to appear unresponsive, failing to recognize its name, but this is not a sign of a loss of mental faculties. Equally, the fact that an older dog soils indoors is not necessarily an indicator that it is confused—it may simply have been in too much pain to get outdoors easily. Yet there can be a recognizable mental deterioration in older dogs that is most likely to manifest itself by separation anxiety at night. An affected individual will become very distressed when left on its own at this stage, barking repeatedly. Palliative veterinary treatment can help in this case. Reassurance from you can also be helpful, and it may be a matter of leaving a low-wattage, low-energy light on to help your pet overcome its fears.

The importance of training

Dogs appreciate having a set routine to their daily lives, with meals and walks taking place at regular times of day, though they can also be quite adaptable when circumstances warrant it. However, it is essential for your dog's happiness, whatever your usual routine, that you train it to follow certain basic instructions.

Timely reminder Your dog will soon come to find you if you are late taking it out for a walk. Some will even learn to bring you their leash as a reminder.

Walking on a leash This Brussels Terrier has been trained to walk well on a leash and not pull ahead.

The need for training

There are certain basic things that you need to teach your dog. It must learn to come when called, to sit on command, and to walk well on a leash. Your pet will also need to be housebroken and must easily give up objects when told to drop them (see page 33). While it is certainly true that young dogs tend to learn more quickly, there is no reason why older dogs should not be able to learn. If you are having difficulty training your dog, you can seek help from a professional dog trainer on a one-to-one basis or sign up for a dog-training class. The sooner you seek advice, the quicker you can overcome the problem.

Teaching your dog

Although it may not always appear to be the case, your dog will be eager to win your approval. Training works much better if you give your pet plenty of encouragement when it responds as required. Do not scold it, because this will undermine its confidence. Break up training sessions so that they are relatively short, as the dog will learn more effectively under these circumstances.

Advice for success

It helps to carry out training in a relatively quiet environment, to keep your pet from getting distracted. This will help its concentration. Build up gradually, being careful not to rush your dog. Once your dog has learned to sit, for example, you can then teach it to stay.

TIP
- *Calmness and consistency are vital for successful training.*

Independent nature
Some puppies are naturally more obedient than others. Shar-Peis and their relatives, the Chow Chows, can be difficult to train.

Routine learning

Try to include a training message as part of the dog's regular routine, rather than carrying out two or three short training sessions every day. For example, from an early age encourage your pet to sit before placing its food bowl on the floor. While it may not present a major problem to have a small puppy jumping around, it can become dangerous if you have a large Great Dane springing up at you to get a taste of its food.

Bonding

It is worth remembering that while training has a function in terms of encouraging good canine behavior, it also provides the opportunity to build the relationship between you and your pet, deepening the bond between you. With this in mind, it is also important that other members of the family help with training, so your pet will not end up being focused entirely on you and your instructions.

SAFETY FIRST
Choose a quiet location to let your dog off the leash for the first time, far away from roads.

Agility training

For sheer excitement, agility competitions are hard to beat, whether as a competitor running alongside your dog or as a spectator. All types of dogs can take part, both pedigree and crossbreeds, competing over a varied course with a range of obstacles that must be negotiated against the clock.

Obstacles Dogs taking part in agility contests are expected to negotiate a range of obstacles.

Competition origins

The idea of canine agility competitions was first adopted during the late 1970s at the famous Crufts dog show, held in London, England. The early courses were designed to be similar to a show-jumping course for horses. Since then, it has spread to become a worldwide sport. There is no standard course, and the various organizations involved operate under their own rules. Dogs may be divided on the basis of their size, as well as on the grounds of experience. The general aim is to complete the course as quickly as possible, with a minimum number of faults. Penalties can be imposed for missing obstacles or knocking them over, as well as for being too slow.

WEAVING

This is one of the most difficult obstacles for a dog to master in an agility course. It must enter with the first pole to its left-hand shoulder and then twist and turn in sequence between all the remaining poles, without missing any. There can be up to a dozen, with the space between each one being about 20 in. (51 cm).

Starting training

Although training often starts with young dogs, it is very important to begin with basic equipment, scaling back and adjusting the height of the jumps, for example, so the dog will not injure itself. Although it is possible to teach your dog at home, it is more common for would-be participants in agility competitions to join a local club, where they can benefit from the assistance of more experienced members. Since you will need to be running alongside your dog giving instructions, with the typical agility course extending over an area of 100 × 100 ft. (30 × 30 m), you may need to train yourself to ensure that you can keep up with your pet. It is also vital that you familiarize yourself with the layout of the course before the competition.

Pausing for breath

A wide variety of obstacles make up the agility course. It is not necessarily all about speed, because there may be a pause table or a pause box. Here, the dog is expected to rest, typically for five seconds, either lying down or sitting.

Ladders and planks

Obstacles that must be climbed are an integral part of an agility course. These may take the form of two ramps, creating an A-shape, or a dog walk, which is a plank with two other planks leading up and down from it. There are crossovers, too, with a range of different planks leading up and down from a platform requiring the dog to negotiate the correct pairing depending on the type of competition. Even more tricky is the seesaw, where the dog runs up one side, then its weight tilts the seesaw down and the dog runs down the other side. It takes slighter longer for smaller dogs to tilt this plank because they weigh less, so they are given extra time to complete the course.

Tunnels

Terrier-type competitors are well suited to tunnels. The tunnel may be freestanding so that the dog can get through easily, either in a straight line or curves. The other form, known as a collapsed tunnel, has fabric lying along its length, so the dog needs to wriggle and burrow its way through.

Jumps

The arrangement of the bars in the jumps is variable. They may be one above the other or they could be at an angle, creating a spread jump. In the case of a panel jump, the bars are replaced with a panel extending up from the ground. Its height will be adjusted according to the height of the dog.

Tire jump The canine contestant is expected to jump through the hoop—the center of the tire, in this case.

Behavior when traveling

As our lives have changed and we travel more, so have the lives of our closest companions. Whether we are flying, sailing, or even just going on a car trip, our dogs often accompany us. They may react differently, depending on their surroundings, compared to when they are at home.

Small breeds are more vulnerable Small dogs such as this Shih Tzu will find it harder to swim in strong currents and may get into trouble quickly in the water.

Car travel

Some dogs are very nervous about traveling by car, but provided that you familiarize your pet with this experience regularly from a young age, you should encounter few, if any, problems. This shows the highly adaptable nature of dogs. Even in the case of a dog that has not been used to traveling by car until later in life, it will adapt, although this process may take longer than with a young dog.

Just like people, dogs that are taken out in a vehicle may suffer from motion sickness as a result of the unfamiliar sensations that they encounter. This phase should soon pass, though, and you may be able to prevent it entirely by taking your puppy out for short rides in the car even before it can go out for walks. Avoid feeding your pet beforehand as this increases the likelihood that it will vomit. Keep it confined in a suitable crate, so that it cannot roam about the vehicle and, if it does vomit, the mess will be much easier to clean up, with no damage to the car's upholstery.

Plan ahead Always consider your dog's well-being. Life jackets, for example, are available for dogs taking boat trips, just in case your pet falls overboard. The handle on the back as shown here will mean that you can lift your pet up easily from the water.

HAZARDS IN THE CAR

Safety considerations are important when traveling with your pet. Although many dogs like putting their head out of the window when in a moving car, you should discourage this, as the speed of travel can cause eye ailments. If your pet attempted to push itself farther out of the window, it could also distract you momentarily, leading to a serious accident. There is also a slight risk of your dog being hit by a passing car that comes too close.

Restraining your pet

Being able to confine your dog safely and securely, especially when traveling by car, is essential. A dog will not understand the danger of causing a driver to lose concentration and, in a collision, your pet is likely to suffer a more serious injury if it is not properly restrained—by being thrown against the windshield, for example. Dog guards, crates for small dogs that can be lifted in and out of the vehicles, or even canine seat belts, are all possibilities to consider.

Anticipating hazards

It is always important to try to anticipate hazards to your pet, especially when you are visiting an area that differs significantly from your home. In new surroundings, even an older dog can be at risk, perhaps encountering dangerous creatures, such as venomous snakes, with which it is unfamiliar. Although older dogs are more cautious than puppies—and are less likely to rush up to a snake when they see one for the first time, for example—there is still an element of danger, as the other creature's behavior will be unpredictable. Pay close attention to your dog, call it back to you, and put it on its leash if necessary.

Dangers in the water

A dog that is used to swimming in a lake at home will not be aware of the risk of alligators, which may lurk in wait in warmer climates—in such vacation destinations as Florida, for example. This risk is significant; these particular reptiles prey readily on dogs and you will have little chance of rescuing your pet if it is seized by an alligator. The landscape may hold other hazards that your pet cannot anticipate, ranging from fast-flowing currents around jetties to thin ice on ponds. Remember that your pet will behave as it would do at home, and take precautions as necessary.

SAFETY FIRST

Never leave your dog on its own in a locked vehicle, as the temperature within can rise to a fatal level within minutes.

Snowbound This Wire-haired Fox Terrier is encountering snow for the first time and is excited, but it can suffer from the buildup of frozen snow on its body, easily becoming chilled. A coat is ideal for most dogs in freezing temperatures.

Life in
the litter

Toys for
puppies

Puppies
at play

Interacting
with older dogs

Venturing out

Chewing

Leaving
the litter

74

Young at Heart

Understanding your puppy

Newborn
puppies

Tail chasing

Test of
strength

Nervousness

Easing
worries

Growing
puppies

Life in the litter

While the puppies still live with each other and their mother in their litter, they learn about pack hierarchy—a concept that will shape the young dog's life even once it leaves its family, and guide how it behaves and interacts in the wider world.

Rough play

As the time for weaning approaches (see page 80), puppies start to become more lively. They will be very eager to play, both with each other and with their mother. Puppies use their mouths to explore a variety of objects, and they often play quite roughly with each other. The presence of surprisingly sharp teeth means that they may inflict a painful bite while playing, although this is entirely unintentional.

TIP

- *Don't worry that the bitch is being rough with her puppies; being able to control her offspring helps keep them safe.*

Learning through play
Puppies develop their agility and coordination by playing with each other. Here, a young West Highland White puppy climbs on top of its littermate.

Learning their own strength

Although puppies rarely draw blood in a game, an individual will squeal in pain and withdraw whimpering from an encounter if it has been hurt. Before too long, perhaps as a result of being nipped by other puppies, the youngsters learn their own strength and adjust their play rituals accordingly. There are certain parts of the body where a bite is more painful, with one of the most sensitive areas being the tip of the nose. This area of the body has a high concentration of nerve endings in dogs, as it serves to detect scents. Most often, it is more exposed areas such as the ears and the tip of the tail that are grabbed by another excited puppy during play. The pups may also wrestle with each other, and their sharp claws can make painful scratches across their exposed underparts.

Tolerant parenting This Staffordshire Bull Terrier mother is under painful attack from two of her puppies, which are only six weeks old. While one is aiming at her nose, the other is biting the skin of her neck.

Multidog household

Although bitches tend to be most tolerant toward their own puppies, other dogs in the household may be similarly well disposed toward them. However, there is no guarantee of this, so close supervision is essential once the puppies are active. There may be flashpoints as they grow older as well, especially at mealtimes. Dogs should ideally be kept apart at meals, because if a younger dog tries to sneak in and take an older dog's food, this could meet with an aggressive response. After an encounter of this type, however, puppies will generally learn not to intrude, but to wait to eat at a later stage. Similar behavior is seen in wolf packs, where the food is divided up among pack members after a kill; the younger members of the pack may have to wait for the more dominant pack members to finish before they can feed.

Encounters with strangers

On their first walks, young dogs can become quite excitable. If two dogs of this age meet, they will usually play together without problems. But if an older individual is subjected to regular harassment and does not wish to engage, then it is likely to growl a warning, before chasing the younger dog away quite aggressively over a short distance.

A firm message Puppies must be disciplined firmly by their mother if they do not refrain from behavior that they have previously been warned about.

Staying in charge This bitch feels the need to issue a stern warning to her puppy, who is now well grown. She grasps the puppy's jaws in hers, clamping them shut. This communicates a very clear message about her greater strength and higher social ranking in the canine hierarchy.

Newborn puppies

Although they are blind at first, with their eyes closed, and unable to hear, newborn puppies are adept at getting exactly what they need to survive—food and warmth.

Open eyes Puppies' eyes open sometime after about ten days.

Vigilant mother If one of her young puppies strays, this Dalmatian mother will retrieve it, gently picking it up and carrying it in her mouth.

Movement Puppies have a very limited ability to move at first, but they will start feeding within half an hour of being born, and will gradually become more athletic.

Sleeping close for warmth

Puppies lose heat very easily, partly because they have a high surface area relative to their volume. They are also incapable of regulating their body heat effectively, compared with adult dogs. They cannot shiver—a reflex response that generates heat in adult dogs—nor do they have the ability to raise their fur to trap air close to the skin, which is then warmed by body heat and provides insulation. This susceptibility to cold is why young puppies sleep together—collectively they overcome their tendency to lose heat quickly. If the puppies become too hot, however, then they roll apart.

SAFETY FIRST

If a puppy seems distressed and is moving around the mother a lot without latching on, this may be a sign that it is not feeding well.

Mewing for mom

Young puppies can communicate vocally from an early age. They have a very distinctive "mewing" call, which is only audible over a short distance. The purpose of this call is to attract the attention of their mother, who is likely to be close by. This trait is inherited from wolves and is connected with survival; the call is not likely to be audible to potential predators, helping to ensure the safety of the young wolf cubs or puppies. The young dog will typically lift its head slightly when searching for its mother. If it cannot find her, then it will start crying slightly louder until she can hear him.

HEAT AWARENESS

Young dogs are blind and deaf at birth, but they are able to detect heat, typically from their mother's or their siblings' bodies. In a newborn litter, when one member moves to feed, the others usually follow.

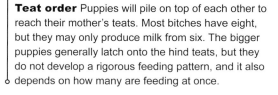

Teat order Puppies will pile on top of each other to reach their mother's teats. Most bitches have eight, but they may only produce milk from six. The bigger puppies generally latch onto the hind teats, but they do not develop a rigorous feeding pattern, and it also depends on how many are feeding at once.

Growing puppies

As puppies grow older, they start to move around more and explore their immediate environment. They also interact more with each other. In the wild, this is a crucial phase, as it helps the young dogs start learning skills essential to their survival.

Time to wean

In the case of domestic dogs, the mother looks after the puppies at first, rearing them on her own. She remains in close attendance for the first three weeks of their lives, by which time, they will start to be more mobile. Up until the age of about six weeks, she will allow them to suckle on demand, but after that point they are ready to be weaned onto solid food. From her perspective, this is when their first set of teeth start to emerge, and suckling becomes painful for her. By deterring them from doing this, she causes her milk production to slow down and eventually stop.

SAFETY FIRST

If the mother is reluctant to let her puppies suckle she may have inflamed mammary glands— an indication of mastitis.

Enough is enough
Once this Cavalier King Charles Spaniel bitch has had enough of her puppies suckling, she will simply walk away.

Regurgitation

As the milk flow stops, the mother will start to engage in what may appear a rather worrying pattern of behavior. However, it will ultimately help her puppies to be able to digest solid food. She eats her food normally and then returns to the puppies, appearing to be fine. Without any warning, she will then start retching, bringing up her meal. This vomiting is carried out deliberately close to her puppies.

Help with digestion

The puppies start to clean up the mess, eating the regurgitated and partially digested food. Unpleasant though this behavior seems to us, it is quite normal for pet dogs, and is commonplace among wild dogs, too. By acting in this way, the bitch is actually helping the puppies to start digesting solid food, which has already been partially broken down by her own digestive system.

Growing up

All puppies are actually of a similar size when they are born, whether they are Chihuahuas or Great Danes but, after birth, there is a marked difference in their growth rates, with bigger breeds growing proportionately faster. Whatever the breed, it is likely to take at least 18 months until a dog is fully grown.

Close bonds

As puppies grow up, the bonds established during puppyhood remain. If you are looking for two dogs, then choose littermates for this reason (bearing in mind that they will need to be neutered if they are different sexes). Watch their behavior closely, and you are likely to see that one individual is more forceful than the other. This is unlikely to be a problem, though; the pack order has been established and will not be challenged later on. Introducing two young dogs that do not know each other already will call for a period of adjustment for all parties, yourself included.

Gaining independence When they are ready, young puppies will start to sniff around their immediate environment and begin to wander away from their mother. If a puppy encounters difficulties, though, it will call to attract her (see page 79).

Emerging character

Many people look for individual characteristics when choosing a puppy but, in reality, the differences between dogs are not especially marked at this early stage in life. Much will depend on when a puppy last slept or had a meal—both these activities will influence its behavior and, therefore, its perceived character at the time it is being viewed. Male puppies can sometimes be a little bolder and possibly more assertive than females. The young dog's experiences as it grows up will be much more significant in forming its character in the long run.

Time for development Do not worry if the puppies appear clumsy and have difficulty standing, as they take time to develop coordination. It will also take time for them to recognize their names—this is only likely to occur after weaning. This litter of Dachshunds is several weeks old.

Puppies at play

The behavior of puppies changes as they grow older. They are characterized by their playfulness, combined with high energy levels. Play is an essential part of learning and should be encouraged, but do watch out for hidden dangers.

Hazardous time

Puppies have playful, inquisitive natures, which allow them to gain information about the world around them through experimentation and exploration. However, they do not possess the instinctive caution of an adult dog, and this can lead them into danger. It is no coincidence that puppies are especially likely to sustain snake bites—usually because they get too close to one of these reptiles. Puppies are also more inclined to chew on and swallow objects and may end up with internal impactions as a result; swallowing items such as socks and hosiery, for example, may necessitate surgery. Take care with toys as well, because if these are too small, they could make your puppy choke.

What's out there?
These Papillon puppies are inquisitive and alert, eager to find out about the world around them.

Play fighting

Here you can see a play fight taking place between two young Labrador Retriever puppies (right). Each dog is picking up on visual clues from its opponent, as well as vocalizations. Even at this age, puppies are capable of inflicting serious injuries on each other in a fight. However, they very rarely hurt each other; it is very much a matter of testing each other's strength at this stage, although this type of play is energy-sapping for them. After a workout like this, both puppies are likely to fall fast asleep.

A useful purpose
Play fighting is not just fun—it also helps puppies such as these Labrador Retrievers improve their agility and coordination.

Up for a game

Just like adult dogs, puppies communicate both verbally and visually, although there will be a different emphasis on the type of communication a young dog uses, compared to an older one. For example, the playful nature of puppies means they use the "play bow" gesture frequently, both with their owner and also with other dogs that they know well. They crouch down with their front legs extended and their hindquarters raised. When a toy is thrown, the young dog will then spring up and chase it.

SAFETY FIRST

Never throw a stick for a dog to chase—it could spear the roof of the mouth or tongue if your pet stumbles.

Power balance The upper puppy is aiming to maintain its position and keep its companion pinned to the ground. There is a possibility that the puppy on its back will be able to regain the initiative and throw its littermate off-balance by rolling on top of it.

Safe to chew Puppies love to chew objects, even potentially dangerous ones such as electrical wires. Keep your pup safe by providing plenty of objects that are safe to chew on.

Raring to play Boxers rank among the liveliest breeds and are always ready to play. This young Boxer is clearly looking for a game.

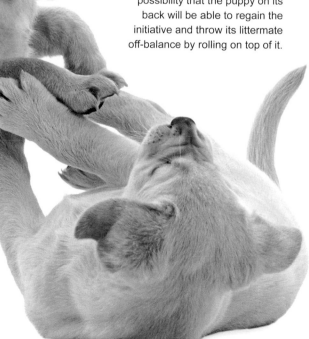

Leaving the litter

Although puppies are rather shy when they are first separated from their mother and littermates, they are adaptable by nature and will settle relatively quickly in unfamiliar surroundings, especially once they become used to a new routine.

Settling in

You can help your new puppy settle in and gain confidence by adopting a positive tone when calling your pet. Puppies are naturally enthusiastic and will gain confidence from the tone of your voice. However, you should aim to strike a balance and not let your pet become overconfident—if this happens you may end up in a situation where the puppy ignores your commands and gets itself into a dangerous position. This is why early basic training is so important (see pages 68–69), especially teaching your puppy to come back to you when called (see opposite). If you see your pet trying to cross a street without you, for example, you can call it back to you, keeping it safe.

Cautiously confident This puppy looks confident and alert, with its ears forward, although its slightly drooping tail suggests that it may not be completely sure of itself.

Living with others If you have other pets, the new puppy will have to learn to get along with them. This puppy runs the risk of being scratched by the kitten—a mistake he may not repeat.

SAFETY FIRST

A young puppy faces many possible dangers, so watch over your pet carefully, especially when you start going out for walks.

Answering to its name

The name that you choose for your pet is only significant to you; if you always talk to your puppy using its name, it will soon learn to recognize the sound. To avoid confusion, don't use the same name for your puppy as for another member of the household. Call your puppy back to you regularly throughout the day, both when you are in the same room and from elsewhere in the house. Do this in the backyard, too; puppies learn best by repetition. You are aiming for a situation where the puppy will come to you almost instinctively when called. When training a dog, remember that its breed may make a difference in the techniques that will work best. Whatever the breed, consistency and repetition are very important during training.

Battle of wills This young Cavalier King Charles puppy has its own ideas when it comes to walking on the leash. It is pulling in the opposite direction from the way the owner intends it to walk.

Overconfidence English Bull Terriers such as this one can be naturally very confident when meeting other dogs; this can sometimes lead to conflict.

Confidence issues during training

Confidence can exert itself in undesirable ways during the training process when the young dog decides that it is not going to cooperate. There is no point in getting angry when your puppy fails to respond as required, because it may simply be unclear about what the instruction is. Also, you do not want to undermine its confidence—simply repeat the training procedure. One key to success with training—and keeping your puppy's confidence up—is not to do it for too long. Short, frequent sessions are much better than a training marathon. Keep going over the basics and build on what your puppy has already learned.

Overconfident breeds

Some breeds are more confident by nature than others, with the English Bull Terrier (left) being a typical example of a confident dog. This can give rise to training difficulties, as the dog may display a strong independent streak. Many guard dogs, such as the various Mastiff breeds, are very determined by nature and this needs to be considered when undertaking their training.

Venturing out

A new world of exploration awaits your puppy out-of-doors, but do keep your pet confined to your backyard until it has completed its vaccinations. Being outside provides a new opportunity to build on the puppy's early training routines.

Housetraining

Your puppy should become familiar with the backyard from very early on; placing your pet outside at regular intervals is a crucial part of housetraining. If you anticipate the times when the puppy is most likely to relieve itself, then hopefully you will only have to clean up after your pet in the home very occasionally, from the outset. This will also help speed up the process of training the dog to ask to go outside, which may otherwise take several months.

Establishing a routine

Start to develop a routine by encouraging your dog to go into the backyard first thing in the morning and then again around lunchtime, in the late afternoon, and during the evening, before finally placing your puppy outside for the last time just before you go to bed. Try to encourage your puppy to relieve itself in one part of the backyard only, preferably on a hard surface where you can clean up and disinfect the area easily.

Burning off energy The backyard provides an ideal location for young dogs to burn off some of their excess energy.

Suitable toys Young dogs in particular will improvise when it comes to toys, especially if there are none available. To ensure their safety, try to provide a range of toys that you know are definitely safe for them.

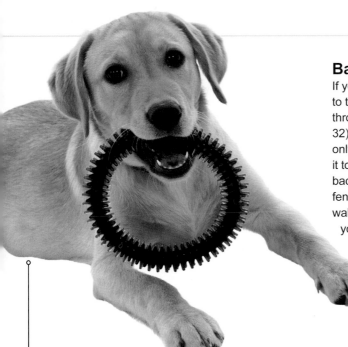

Backyard schooling

If you have a reasonable area of lawn, you can start to teach your puppy to retrieve toys that you have thrown, getting your pet to bring them to you (see page 32). And once your puppy is used to its collar—which only takes a couple of days—you can start to teach it to walk on a leash. This can be done easily in the backyard with few distractions, especially if you have a fence or wall that you can use to help keep the puppy walking in a straight line. Do not be surprised if, at first, your puppy simply rolls onto its back and tries to gnaw on the leash. This is quite common. Before long, it will realize what is expected, though it may still pull in different directions, depending on where it has detected an interesting scent.

A gentle touch This Labrador Retriever is enjoying chewing on a toy. If you want to retrieve the toy, do not pull, as this could injure the mouth. Instead, teach it to drop on command (see page 33).

TIP

- *Puppies can prove more responsive to training on some days than others.*

Encounters with wildlife

Unfortunately, young dogs are not always aware of the dangers lurking in backyards, and this can have serious consequences. In warmer weather, puppies may snap at bees and wasps, not understanding the risk of being stung. A sting in the mouth, especially in the vicinity of the throat, can be very serious because the tissue there will swell up, cutting off the puppy's air supply. Should your pet suddenly have difficulty breathing after playing outside, seek veterinary advice immediately. Try to keep the airway open at all costs, following advice from your veterinarian.

Equally alarming is your puppy foaming at the mouth. This could indicate that the young dog has grabbed hold of a toad in the yard. Toads have toxic skin secretions that help protect them from would-be predators, and this may be responsible for the puppy's extreme salivation. Again, seek veterinary advice urgently. Puppies tend to learn quickly from experiences of this type and will likely not interfere with such creatures in the future. Try to acquaint yourself with other possible wildlife dangers in the area where you live.

Playing alone This young Beagle is enjoying a game with a ball. Its ears are pulled forward, and its tail is raised, along with a front paw. Young dogs may play by themselves for some time outdoors. You should ensure that any ball is too large to be swallowed.

Nervousness

The body language of a nervous puppy is very different from that of a confident puppy. A number of factors can make an otherwise well-balanced puppy nervous. It is important to stay alert to these and encourage your dog to overcome its fears whenever possible.

Nighttime anxiety

Puppies tend to be nervous when they are separated from their family group. Initially, while you are around, the young dog will show few, if any, signs of distress. However, this may change when you leave the puppy on its own to go to bed. In this case, it will show its distress by whining repeatedly, seeking reassurance. This is the only situation of this type where the best advice is to ignore your pet. Ultimately, it will settle down. If you relent and try to comfort it, this scenario will be repeated every night, because the puppy has learned that whimpering in this way gets your attention.

Although letting your puppy sleep in your bedroom may seem like a short-term solution, do not be tempted to do this. It will become almost impossible to evict your pet at a later stage, and then you risk facing fleas in your room, torn bedcovers, and even being forced out of your own bed. This is an example of starting as you mean to finish and not giving your dog confusing mixed messages.

Nervous older dogs Older dogs may be nervous, too, often because of bad experiences in the past. Rescued dogs that may have been the victims of mistreatment will need plenty of understanding. This dog is clearly feeling uncertain, with one ear drawn back and a nervous look in its eye.

GETTING USED TO CAR TRAVEL
Puppies will be not be used to traveling in a moving vehicle and may suffer from nervousness as well as travel sickness at first. Take your pet out on short journeys to begin with, even before it goes out for walks, to get it used to this experience.

Visiting the veterinarian

Puppies will often display signs of nervousness, even if there is no obvious cause. One of the first situations where you are likely to encounter this type of behavior is when you visit the veterinarian with your new pet for the first time. The combination of the journey, the noise, and the scent of other dogs, plus an encounter with a stranger, may cause your puppy to become withdrawn and uncooperative. It is important to reassure your pet that nothing harmful is going to happen. Most veterinarians will take time to reassure the puppy so that it does not become fearful about visiting the vet in the future (see pages 64–65).

Typical indicators

The signs of nervousness are usually consistent, regardless of the cause. The dog will tend to crouch down, pulling its ears back and lowering them, as well as tucking its tail between its hind legs, while it watches closely whatever it was that made it nervous. It may also try to escape from the perceived danger, heading off in the opposite direction if possible. Should your pet feel trapped or abandoned, it will likely start to whine as well.

SAFETY FIRST

Remember that there may be certain "triggers" that remind rescue dogs of their past and will cause them to become very distressed.

Showing submission
By lowering itself, this puppy is signaling that it is not a threat to anyone approaching.

Eye contact This puppy is showing its lack of confidence in its eyes, and may even avert its gaze. Staring directly at another dog may otherwise be interpreted as a threat.

Friend or stranger? This young crossbred dog is clearly nervous about its feline companion. A puppy reared in a home on its own and suddenly encountering a cat for the first time in the backyard will be unsure whether the other animal represents a threat or not.

Easing worries

The world can be a worrying and frightening place for a young puppy isolated in unfamiliar surroundings, away from where it grew up. It is very important to provide reassurance, especially at first, so that it feels comforted and does not carry this worry with it throughout its life.

Worry-free training

Some breeds, such as the Italian Greyhound, tend to give more of an appearance of worrying, which can be seen in their body language. They are more sensitive than many other dogs, and it is important to bear this in mind during the training process (see pages 68–69) and avoid speaking harshly. Dogs must be given clear instructions during training—do not add to your pet's worry by making it confused. Even if you have trained a puppy before, it is important to bear in mind that each one is an individual, and they are likely to learn at different speeds—even members of the same breed. Do not become impatient if your new pet does not appear to be learning as quickly as its predecessor. Learning in dogs is rarely a smooth progression, but often moves forward in sudden leaps!

SAFETY FIRST

Do not forget that dogs will sometimes shiver not because of the cold, but because they are frightened.

Seriously worried The whole posture of this Dachshund puppy indicates that it is worried, with its body hunched and head held down. It is not as easy to judge its mood from the position of its ears, though, as these are not particularly expressive or mobile.

Genuine worry? Although a worried dog needs reassurance, you need to be careful that you do not inadvertently teach your dog the wrong lesson, so that it ends up conditioned to display signs of worry because it knows that it will get your affection as a result.

Whites of the eyes
Much of this puppy's worried demeanor is expressed in its eyes. Here the eyes are fixed on the object of concern, and the whites are even visible.

Not real worry Some dogs, especially members of the Mastiff group such as this Pug, appear permanently worried due to the wrinkled skin on their forehead.

Rooted to the spot When a puppy is very unsure of itself, it will not attempt to run off in fear, but will instead remain rooted to the spot.

TIP

• *Loud noises and flashes of light caused by fireworks or thunderstorms can be very distressing for all dogs, regardless of age; keep the drapes closed to minimize this source of worry.*

When worry is a worry
Puppies generally adapt very quickly, but this may not hold true in the case of a young rescue dog that has been mistreated. Such dogs may appear very worried, cowering away if in close proximity to a man or woman that reminds them of their previous owner. In fact, it is not uncommon for such dogs to develop a distinctive gender bias based on their previous experiences. This might make them unsuitable as family pets. Such individuals can often be won over if you are patient and prepared to work intensively with them, perhaps with a canine behaviorist, to isolate and address the underlying problems.

Extreme worry
Severe worry can lead to flashes of aggression, although generally in such cases a dog will go through warning stages, growling with increasing intensity before reacting violently. This situation may resolve itself, as the worried dog will likely try to withdraw and escape at the earliest opportunity. In extreme cases, dogs may even soil indoors if they are very worried or distressed.

Interacting with older dogs

It is remarkable just how tolerant some older dogs can be when they meet energetic puppies. Indeed, as long as they are introduced to each other carefully, a young individual should settle well in a house with an established older dog.

A natural partnership

Many older dogs appear to empathize with younger dogs, being remarkably well disposed toward them, even if they are meeting for the first time. They are fairly unlikely to react aggressively—something they might do with a dog of a similar age. This may be because a young dog represents no threat to them.

Although an older individual might not actively encourage the younger dog to play, it may react in a playful manner if invited to do so by its younger companion. It is most likely to respond by chasing the young dog around, although not in an aggressive way. The older dog will often join in with the puppy's play—for example, if the young dog is playing with a toy, then its companion might steal the toy, causing the puppy to give chase.

Introducing a new puppy

If you decide that you want to have two dogs instead of only one, it will be much easier if you opt for a young puppy to live alongside an older dog, rather than introducing an older dog of a similar age to your existing pet. The status of both individuals is then predefined, and the risk of any major conflict is ruled out, because the older dog is dominant.

The gender of the dogs is not especially significant, although dogs of some breeds can be less friendly than bitches. This tends to apply in the case of larger, more assertive breeds such as the Doberman. Much depends on the individual temperaments of the dogs concerned, however, and a younger dog is more likely to be accepted by an older, established individual if the dogs are introduced regularly beforehand—for example, while out for a walk. The established individual will not then be made to feel vulnerable on home territory. The addition of a puppy to a household often encourages the older dog to become more lively and playful. Be prepared to step in and separate the dogs, though, if the puppy will not leave its older companion alone.

Deferential behavior
This young Beagle is reaching up toward the face of the adult Lurcher. The young dog is showing its older companion that he represents no threat.

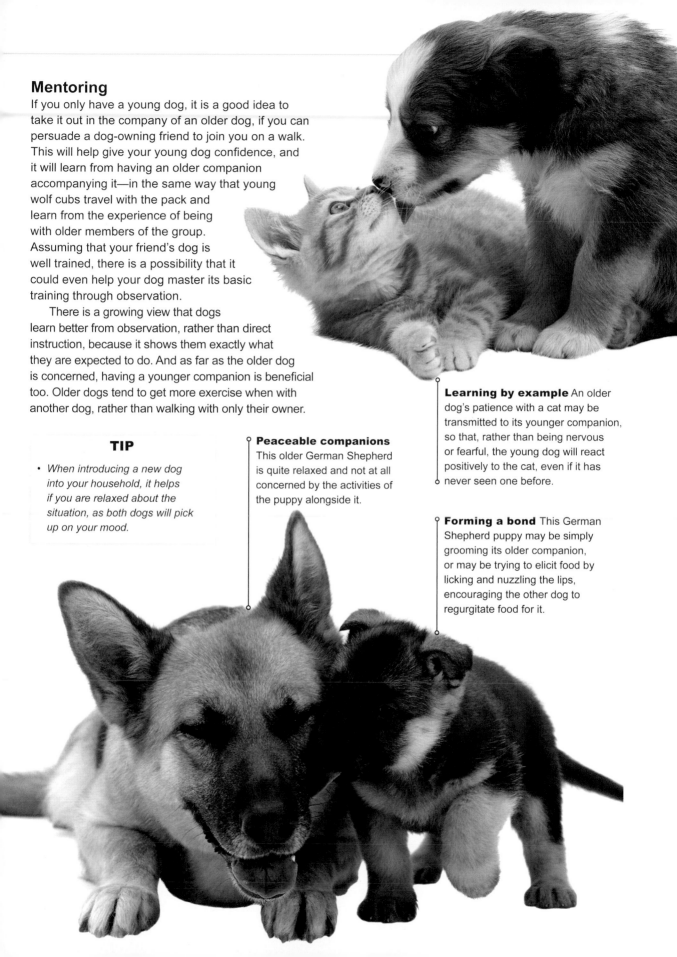

Mentoring

If you only have a young dog, it is a good idea to take it out in the company of an older dog, if you can persuade a dog-owning friend to join you on a walk. This will help give your young dog confidence, and it will learn from having an older companion accompanying it—in the same way that young wolf cubs travel with the pack and learn from the experience of being with older members of the group. Assuming that your friend's dog is well trained, there is a possibility that it could even help your dog master its basic training through observation.

There is a growing view that dogs learn better from observation, rather than direct instruction, because it shows them exactly what they are expected to do. And as far as the older dog is concerned, having a younger companion is beneficial too. Older dogs tend to get more exercise when with another dog, rather than walking with only their owner.

TIP

- When introducing a new dog into your household, it helps if you are relaxed about the situation, as both dogs will pick up on your mood.

Peaceable companions This older German Shepherd is quite relaxed and not at all concerned by the activities of the puppy alongside it.

Learning by example An older dog's patience with a cat may be transmitted to its younger companion, so that, rather than being nervous or fearful, the young dog will react positively to the cat, even if it has never seen one before.

Forming a bond This German Shepherd puppy may be simply grooming its older companion, or may be trying to elicit food by licking and nuzzling the lips, encouraging the other dog to regurgitate food for it.

Toys for puppies

A puppy rarely misses the opportunity to play, unless it is feeling sick. It may become so involved that it will continue playing until almost literally falling asleep in the middle of the game. Puppies will use any toys you provide, or else improvise—so be careful what you leave lying around!

Choosing toys

An ever-increasing array of toys—some of which claim to test your dog's intelligence, and others that they will boost its fitness—is now available. It is worth remembering that dog toys need to be robust, especially for puppies that may destroy them by treating them as substitutes for chews. Match the size of the toy to the size of your puppy; otherwise, it might restrict the game.

Improvisation

When selecting toys, you also need to bear in mind the area where they will be played with. A frisbee, for example, could easily be lost over a backyard fence. Young dogs are naturally inventive and can make up their own games—using fallen apples as disposable balls, for example. This is an area where the individuality of particular puppies will become apparent and, once a puppy has developed its own game, such as letting a ball roll down a hill and chasing it, the behavior will continue as it grows up. The dog's power of memory also means that your pet will start playing with apples again once they start falling from the tree the following year.

Having a ball This Pug puppy is focusing on the toy in front of it, which it can pick up without difficulty in its wide jaws. It may also use its feet to manipulate the ball.

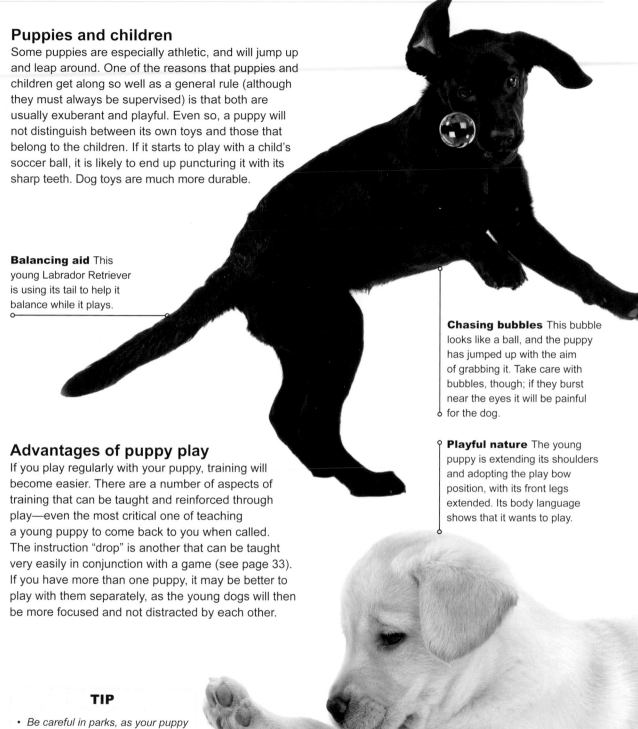

Puppies and children

Some puppies are especially athletic, and will jump up and leap around. One of the reasons that puppies and children get along so well as a general rule (although they must always be supervised) is that both are usually exuberant and playful. Even so, a puppy will not distinguish between its own toys and those that belong to the children. If it starts to play with a child's soccer ball, it is likely to end up puncturing it with its sharp teeth. Dog toys are much more durable.

Balancing aid This young Labrador Retriever is using its tail to help it balance while it plays.

Chasing bubbles This bubble looks like a ball, and the puppy has jumped up with the aim of grabbing it. Take care with bubbles, though; if they burst near the eyes it will be painful for the dog.

Advantages of puppy play

If you play regularly with your puppy, training will become easier. There are a number of aspects of training that can be taught and reinforced through play—even the most critical one of teaching a young puppy to come back to you when called. The instruction "drop" is another that can be taught very easily in conjunction with a game (see page 33). If you have more than one puppy, it may be better to play with them separately, as the young dogs will then be more focused and not distracted by each other.

Playful nature The young puppy is extending its shoulders and adopting the play bow position, with its front legs extended. Its body language shows that it wants to play.

TIP

• *Be careful in parks, as your puppy may run up to children, wanting to join in a game with them. If they do play together, ensure that children are gentle with the puppy and do not tease it.*

Chewing

Puppies have an irresistible desire to chew, which is partially linked to the teething process, but it can become a source of conflict in the home if items of clothing or other objects are damaged as a consequence. The only certain way to prevent this is to keep them out of reach.

Sharing a chew Two Labrador Retriever pups with a chew.

Dog chews

The best way to keep valuable items from being chewed is to provide your puppy with suitable alternatives. In the past, the bones of cattle were used to make dog chews, but more hygienic options (less likely to attract flies!), can now be bought in pet stores. Just as with toys, puppies will have their individual preferences when it comes to chews, so be prepared to experiment a little at first. It is important to try to match the size of the chew to the size of the puppy, so that the young dog can pick it up and carry it around easily. Both temporary (rawhide) and more permanent (rubber) chews are available.

SAFETY FIRST

Keep your puppy from eating too much of a rawhide chew, as this may lead to a digestive upset.

Introducing the chew

Your puppy will need to realize that the chew belongs to it, and intended to be played with and used. Start by calling your puppy over to you and letting it sniff the chew, especially if it is made of rawhide, as the scent is likely to attract the dog's interest. Then throw the chew a short distance across the floor, to encourage the puppy to run after it. You may also want to have a tug-of-war with your pet involving the chew, as this will emphasize to the puppy that it is a toy. You can also use the chew as a toy to be retrieved over a longer distance, encouraging your pet to sniff it out from where you have hidden it.

Staying in control As with toys, puppies can become possessive about chews. Be prepared to take them away and give them back when you think fit, to avoid this.

TIP

• *Chews can prevent a buildup of tartar on a dog's teeth.*

Getting a grip This young Labrador Retriever shows how dogs use their paws like hands to hold onto items when chewing them. Keep electrical wires disconnected and concealed, as far as possible, to stop your dog from gnawing on them, which could be very dangerous.

Chewing posture Dogs usually lie down on their chest in this way when chewing objects.

Teething aids

Puppies are not very good at chewing in the period up to the age of about six months. This is because, at this stage, they are in the process of losing their first set of teeth—often called "milk teeth." These are replaced by permanent teeth, which will last for the rest of their lives. Unfortunately, just as for children, the process of teething can be intensely painful, and at this stage the young dog will try to chew on anything available for some relief. At this time, try to keep a range of different chews readily available in various parts of your home—for example, in your dog's bed. This should keep your teething dog from chewing things you'd rather it didn't.

When the adult teeth do come through, these will include special carnassial teeth, formed by the first lower molar and the last upper premolar in each jaw. These shearing teeth are designed for meat but can cut through all kinds of items very effectively.

Shoe lovers

Dogs love chewing shoes, especially those made of leather. Shoes may also be reassuring, because they carry the odor of their owner, and even if this is not detectable to us it will be to the dog. Most dogs pass through a shoe-chewing phase while teething (see above) but for some this preference will not end when the new teeth emerge. The best way to prevent this annoying (and potentially expensive) habit is simply to keep your shoes away from the dog.

Not the dog's fault There is little point in getting angry with a puppy that has stolen a shoe. You need to keep such items out of reach.

Test of strength

Young puppies will test their strength regularly in tug-of-war type contests. This behavior starts before weaning, soon after puppies are able to move around easily. Broad-mouthed dogs, such as Staffordshire Bull Terriers, tend to come out on top in such battles.

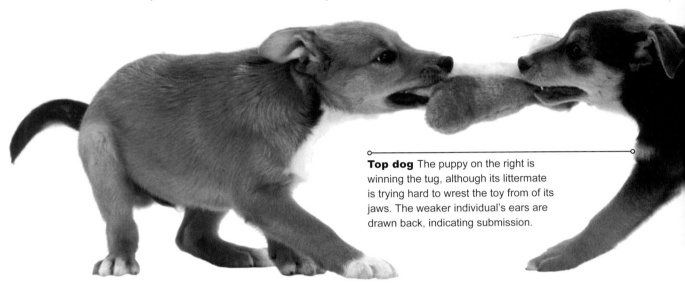

Top dog The puppy on the right is winning the tug, although its littermate is trying hard to wrest the toy from of its jaws. The weaker individual's ears are drawn back, indicating submission.

Good toys to use

Dogs can make use of a variety of toys to play in this way, but you should encourage them to use something soft and smooth that will not damage their mouths. This might be an item that can double as a chew toy and something for your pet to chase after when thrown.

Digging in A Jack Russell puppy uses its powerful hind legs in a tug-of-war.

Behavioral parallels

All puppies engage in this type of tugging behavior, and its origins may lie in the hunting behavior of wolves. Members of the wolf pack sometimes find it difficult to strip meat off the bones of their prey but, by tugging at it, they can break down pieces of the carcass more easily. The combatants eat pieces of meat during this process, pulling chunks off as they tear the joints apart. They may then settle down to gnaw on the bones. Chewing bones keeps the wolves' teeth in good condition by preventing a buildup of tartar. In place of bones (which you should never offer to pet dogs), domestic dogs will typically settle down to chew on the tug toy after an energetic game.

SAFETY FIRST

Do not try to wrestle an item out of your dog's mouth. Instead, control the puppy and carefully open its jaws (see page 33).

Intense duel

The tug-of-war serves another purpose, as it provides young dogs with a means of testing their strength against their littermates, thereby establishing a pack order (see page 76). Typically just two individuals are involved, although other puppies may attempt to join them. This will be resented by both combatants, and they will express their feelings by growling loudly in an intimidating manner. This is usually adequate to deter the intruders. Other members of the litter will usually ignore battling puppies, unless they find themselves in the path of a contest and have to move out of the way. The mother is also unlikely to interfere. As they wrestle over the object, both dogs will likely be growling in a fairly even tone. The growls are usually uttered in conjunction with the rhythm of their movements as they pull. There is no risk of biting, since to do so would require one dog to relinquish its grip.

Development of the play bow

It is easy to see how the play bow gesture may have originated, based on the way that puppies participate in tug-of-war contests, lowering their front legs in this distinctive manner.

Progress of the battle

A tug-of-war contest usually follows a very distinctive pattern. One of the young dogs picks up the toy or object, then the other individual moves in quickly and tries to pull it away from its littermate. Depending on their respective strengths, the puppy that first acquired the object may simply stand its ground, while the other bends its forelegs slightly until they are straight and then uses its powerful hindquarters to pull as hard as it can. Under these circumstances, its front legs may even move together, if the dog is gaining ground, pulling its littermate back with it. As in most tests of strength, there is also a psychological component that will be evident if you observe closely. The more dominant individual is likely to stare intently at its rival, with the aim of intimidating the other dog.

TIP

• *A young dog may lose one of its milk teeth when playing in this way, but this is nothing to worry about.*

Tail chasing

Tail chasing is a distinctive behavior associated with young dogs that disappears over the course of time. It can occasionally become a cause for concern, resulting in damage to the tail. This will need to be investigated by a veterinarian, as there could be an underlying medical problem.

Size is significant
Tail-chasing behavior tends to be seen in medium- to large-size puppies, and can develop into a habit which should not be encouraged.

Possible reason
One theory for this behavior is that the puppy chases its tail in tight circles as a way of developing greater flexibility in its back.

Unstable behavior
A puppy may not always be able to stay on its feet when chasing its tail. It tends to behave like this in an open area, where it will be less likely to hurt itself if it falls over.

Reasons—and solutions

There is no clear reason why young dogs chase their tails; it may be a sign that a puppy is feeling isolated, because such behavior is most commonly seen in puppies separated from their littermates that find themselves in new homes. Nevertheless, this behavior may also be observed in members of a litter before they are fully weaned. It may simply be a reflection of the puppy's lively nature and, if it lacks a companion to play with at that stage, it will naturally chase its own tail. This may seem like obsessive behavior, but it is usually nothing to worry about and is a phase that will pass. If you want to deter your pet from acting in this way, the simplest way is just to call it to you and distract it. Try to encourage the dog to switch its attention to a toy, such as a ball, that it can play with by itself. With something else to occupy itself, it is less likely to chase its tail.

Not for all dogs Not all dog breeds are susceptible to tail chasing. The tail shape of some breeds, such as the English Bulldog puppies seen here, means they cannot chase their tails effectively. Their stocky body shape also makes this difficult.

Puppies only

Sometimes, as a puppy spins around trying to grab hold of its tail, it may fall over onto the floor. This is normally nothing to worry about. It may be that your pet simply lost its balance or became giddy. Having caught its tail, a puppy will hold onto it for a few moments and then relinquish its grip, before repeating the procedure again. When two puppies are together, one puppy may occasionally grab another puppy by the tail as part of a game, usually from behind, but again, it will not hold on for very long. In neither case is the dog's tail likely to be injured. An older dog, however, whether it is playing or even fighting, is not likely to grab the tail of another individual, confirming that this is a behavior confined to young dogs.

Medical concerns

There may be occasions when tail chasing is a cause for concern and, in older individuals, it has been linked with epilepsy. It is important not to encourage the dog to act in this way, and to prevent such behavior from becoming habitual. In severe cases, the wearing of an Elizabethan collar, which keeps the dog from reaching its tail, will help break the habit. Such behavior can arise as the result of boredom. Providing chew toys should provide an effective distraction for your pet.

TAIL BITING

If your dog suddenly starts biting repeatedly at the base of its tail, this is a possible sign that its anal glands are blocked. Your veterinarian will be able to empty them easily. These glands produce a unique secretion that is deposited on the dog's feces, which can be recognized by other dogs.

Digging

Scent
detection

Making
a mark

Fighting

Aggression

Out and About
How your dog behaves outside

Livestock

Odd friendships

Meeting other dogs

Out on the street

Lost dogs

Scentmarking

In the countryside

Dogs and other animals

Hostile meetings

Scent detection

Dogs rely on their sense of smell for insights into the world around them (see pages 106–107). However, some dogs—the scenthounds—are better suited than others to obtaining this information, due to their facial structure and body shape.

Specialist sniffers

The dog's most obvious means of detecting scent is via its nostrils. Dogs' sense of smell is vastly superior to ours, as reflected by comparative genetic mapping, which has shown that dogs possess approximately 30 percent more genes relating to their olfactory system than humans. Dogs can also have as many as two billion specialist nerve cells in their nasal passages, whereas we may have as few as 12 million. The relative surface area within the nasal cavities is significantly larger in dogs, as well.

Smelling for survival

Recent investigations have revealed that puppies can actually become accustomed to scents even before they are born. This has been demonstrated by the fact that they will subsequently display a preference for the type of food that their mother ate during her pregnancy. Almost certainly, this trait was inherited from wolves, and it may help young dogs determine what types of food can be eaten safely, adding to their survival skills once they are weaned and living on their own.

Wet nose It is often wrongly assumed that dogs are sick if they display a dry nose, but this is not necessarily the case. Even so, a moist nose does help the dog detect scent molecules more easily. Sniffing flares the flexible nostrils and has a similar effect.

Brain power The dog's reliance on its sense of smell is reflected by its brain structure. The front area of the brain where this information is received, known as the rhinencephalon, is enlarged in proportion to other areas of the brain. It is linked to the nose via the olfactory nerves.

Varying ability

A dog's sense of smell is not a consistent feature, and its scenting ability can vary over time. Dogs are able to detect scents more effectively when they are hungry, and conversely, their olfactory skills are reduced after a recent meal, especially if it contained animal fats of any kind. It is also no coincidence that aniseed oil is used to lay trails for hounds to follow on a drag hunt. This is not because dogs like the smell of aniseed, but because it is a scent they are known to be able to detect very easily.

Detecting airborne scents

Dogs can also detect airborne scents due to the presence of Jacobson's organ, which is located in the roof of the mouth. Male dogs rely on this organ to detect chemical "messengers" called pheromones, which are released in minute quantities by a bitch in heat (see pages 60–61) and carried by the atmosphere. This silent means of communication explains how male dogs in the neighborhood are able to mysteriously track down a bitch who is ready to mate.

WHO'S AROUND?
This Jack Russell Terrier is sniffing at the base of a tree, detecting information about dogs that may have passed by recently and scentmarked here (see pages 106–107).

Smell and be smelled This Basset Hound is perfectly built for following scent trails. However, it is also laying its own distinctive scent path as it walks, due to the presence of sweat glands between the toes.

Long ears The long ears, a feature of the Basset Hound and some other scenthounds, hang down to the ground like drapes, helping to trap scent molecules close to the nose.

Perfectly formed nose The shape of the Basset Hound's nose is ideally suited to its role as a scenthound. It is long and broad, providing a large internal surface area, packed with sensitive olfactory cells for the purpose of detecting scents.

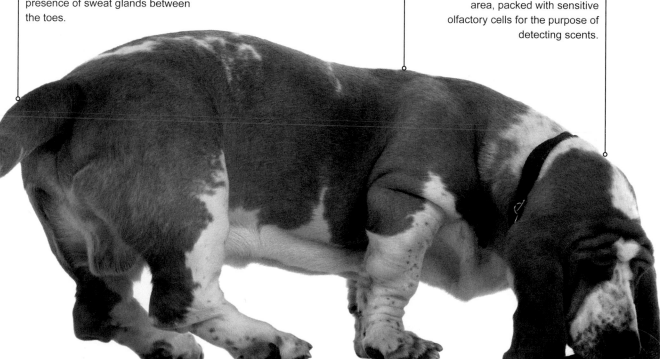

Scentmarking

We understand the world primarily through our senses of sight and hearing. Dogs, however, are able to interpret their surroundings in a completely different way, with their highly developed sense of smell. They scentmark to communicate with other dogs.

Regular marking

Scents linger in the environment, although for how long depends to some extent on the weather conditions. Heavy rain, for example, is very effective at eliminating traces of a scent, simply by diluting it and then washing it away. This is why dogs will frequently scentmark in the same places when out for a walk; they are trying to reinforce their own scent and dilute that of other individuals, clearly marking out what they consider their territory.

A regular pastime

Scentmarking is an activity that is especially common in male dogs. They start to cock their legs as they approach sexual maturity, from about six months of age onward. They will urinate very frequently when out for a walk but do not empty their bladders completely, allowing them to leave their scent at a number of different locations.

Highly developed sense
Dogs can build up a detailed picture of their world using scent.

SAFETY FIRST

Keep your dog's vaccinations up to date, since your pet could contract the illness leptospirosis from sniffing at lamp posts.

Scent mapping

Dogs are not only able to recognize the scents of others of their own kind that have passed through an area. They can also recognize other species, such as foxes or raccoons. This mirrors the way in which wolves determine the location of prey species in their vicinity and also track territorial incursions by members of neighboring packs. Like many predators, wolves roam over large territories, so the ability to home in on the location of potential prey by "scent mapping" is a very useful survival aid. Understanding when events occurred is also important, as this gives a much more detailed picture. Through scent mapping, wolves and dogs are constantly acquiring information about their environment that is totally hidden from us.

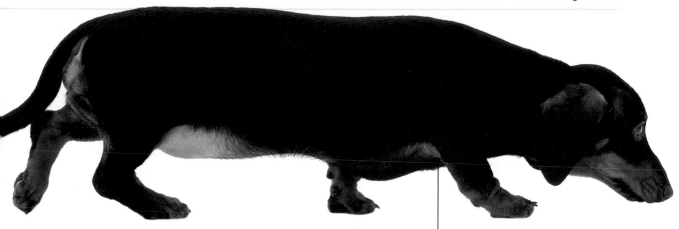

Soothing smells

It is impossible to be sure of the amount of information dogs can process from scents they detect, but studies are revealing different ways in which scents can be used, even at close quarters, for communication purposes. It has been found that lactating bitches, for example, produce a specific pheromone called the "appeasing pheromone." This is released from the vicinity of their mammary glands, can be detected by puppies, and helps to calm them. Tests with an artificial substitute have been found to work on older dogs, and could potentially be used to help calm dogs scared by the noise of fireworks or a visit to a veterinarian. Some other natural odors of plant origin—notably chamomile and lavender—can be detected by dogs and affect their behavior, also providing a calming influence.

On the case This Dachshund is following a scent, walking with its nose close to the ground.

Sniffing for evidence

Dogs deposit their scent on the bodies of other dogs that they meet by rubbing against them, and also by brushing against humans' clothing. This is why your dog will sniff around your legs very thoroughly if you come home after having been in the company of another dog. Scent, as well as visual images, is what helps dogs recognize each other.

TOP SCENTMARKING SPOTS

Dogs tend to choose prominent places for scentmarking, because this is where other dogs are most likely to detect the scent. Common sites for scentmarking include lamp posts, walls, trees, and other vertical surfaces. They may even scentmark inside the house.

Recognition These two crossbred dogs are sniffing each other to see if they are acquainted.

Making a mark

There are a number of ways in which a dog can leave its mark, both around the home and outside, with some of these being more conspicuous than others. They will consist of a combination of visual and olfactory indicators that other dogs will recognize without difficulty.

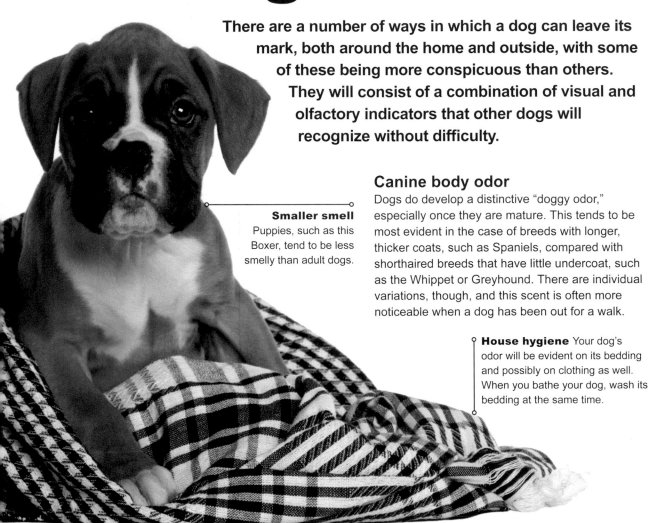

Smaller smell
Puppies, such as this Boxer, tend to be less smelly than adult dogs.

Canine body odor

Dogs do develop a distinctive "doggy odor," especially once they are mature. This tends to be most evident in the case of breeds with longer, thicker coats, such as Spaniels, compared with shorthaired breeds that have little undercoat, such as the Whippet or Greyhound. There are individual variations, though, and this scent is often more noticeable when a dog has been out for a walk.

House hygiene Your dog's odor will be evident on its bedding and possibly on clothing as well. When you bathe your dog, wash its bedding at the same time.

Preparing a bath

Most dogs will benefit from a bath every two or three months to reduce their odor. Obtain some canine shampoo (sold in pet stores), a measuring jug that can serve as a pitcher, and a suitable container that can be used as a bath for your dog outdoors. Avoid using the family bath, as this is not hygienic, but also because your pet's claws can easily scratch the surface, resulting in permanent damage. Choose a warm day, and fill the bath with about 2–3 in. (5–7.5 cm) of tepid water before putting your dog in.

Bathing and drying

Once it has its balance, your pet should relax, especially if the water is not too deep. You can then pour water gently over its coat, starting at the sides of the body and working up to the back, and start working in the shampoo. Leave wetting the head until last and take great care to ensure that no shampoo enters the eyes. It will then need to be rinsed out of the coat. Afterward, stand far back because your dog will shake its coat vigorously, twisting from side to side, as it drives out the droplets of water. You can then rub it down with a clean towel.

SCOOTING

"Scooting" is when a dog drags itself slowly along on the ground, or even indoors across carpeting, moving very slowly with its front feet while keeping its hind legs raised. Such behavior is indicative of blocked anal glands, which are painful and irritating, explaining why the dog will often also nibble intently at the area under its tail. The glands are used to scentmark its feces, and your veterinarian will hopefully be able to clear the blockage easily.

Stick messages

In just the same way that people occasionally carve their initials into a tree, dogs will leave their mark by chewing on sticks. Many dogs will pick these up and instinctively carry them for some distance, pausing and gnawing on them if the opportunity presents itself. By abandoning these sticks along a path, with clear signs that they have been gnawed, they will attract other dogs that pass the same way—with the scent on the sticks acting as a further marker, although this will not be apparent to us. Some dogs will carry suitable sticks relatively long distances when out on a walk, even bringing them home on occasions. At other times, they may drop one stick before picking up another later on during the walk.

Homing instincts

Although there are a number of remarkable stories of lost dogs finding their way home—some dating right back to ancient Rome—dogs generally appear less adept than cats in this regard. Lost dogs do have some skills that they can employ, though, in the same way that a wolf separated from its fellow pack members can find its way back to them. This will be more likely if your pet becomes separated while walking along a route that you often explore together. Providing that it has not rained heavily, the dog will be able to pick up not just its scent, but yours as well. It should also recognize the scenery and may even be able to hear you walking from some distance away, locating you again by a combination of these means.

Stick chewing Young dogs, such as this Beagle puppy, will often chew sticks to ease the pain of new teeth emerging when they are losing their milk teeth.

SAFETY FIRST

Canine odors may not necessarily come from the coat. A sweet, sickly smell in the vicinity of the head could indicate diabetes mellitus. This emanates from the mouth.

Meeting other dogs

Just like people, dogs have their likes and dislikes when it comes to meeting others of their own kind. Some dogs are particularly social, and they send out a clear message of their friendly intent to those that they meet—even from some distance away—using their body language.

SAFETY FIRST

Try not to be overprotective, as it is important that your dog meets other dogs, but keep an eye on how they approach each other.

Balanced relationship
Here both dogs are sitting down, with neither seeking to intimidate the other.

Friendly greeting
These two Springer Spaniel littermates are licking each other's muzzles. This greeting is used by dogs that know each other well.

Shared history

When puppies that have grown up together meet up again soon after having left the litter, they will quickly recognize each other and slip back into a friendly relationship. It is harder to say if they would still know each other after being apart for several months or even years. Certainly, they would be more reserved with each other at first, similar to strange dogs meeting, but perhaps they would then get along well with each other once reacquainted. By this stage, though, they may have grown apart in terms of temperament, since they will have been in different surroundings. This will not necessarily be immediately apparent; the most evident differences are likely to be in levels of training and responsiveness.

Good odor Scent is very important to dogs when they meet, as shown by the way these English Bulldogs are sniffing each other.

Relaxed meeting If they were feeling at all nervous about meeting, the dogs would be more likely to be standing, to allow them to run away easily.

Unpredictable relationships

Dogs of the same breed do not have a natural empathy. In fact some breeds, such as Staffordshire Bull Terriers, may actually be more hostile with each other than if they were meeting a member of a different breed. The respective sizes of the dogs are not significant either, and some dogs simply seem to take a dislike to each other for no obvious reason. The circumstances under which they meet are likely to influence how the dogs view each other. A dog walking on a leash is more likely to be aggressive when confronted by another individual, simply because it is restrained and cannot react as normal in these circumstances. Dogs are actually more likely to get along when meeting off the leash. If one of them does present a threat, one dog can run away easily or, alternatively, they may just pass each other by, after cursory sniffing.

TIP

- *Neighboring dogs may not ever get along, simply because they have become used to defending their territories from each other.*

Aggression

When strange dogs meet, there is always a risk that the encounter will become truly aggressive, although this is not a common occurrence. Some dogs are almost instinctively aggressive, though, so you need to be prepared for this eventuality.

Bowing out This dog is trying to get away from its aggressor, indicating that it is no threat by adopting a very submissive position.

Sequence A dog will go through stylized rituals before it attacks.

Reducing aggression

There are a number of accounts of how ferocious dogs used to be in the past. They were used in battles, as well as becoming feared guardians. However, for over 100 years now, since dogs first entered the show ring, the aim has been to reduce the levels of aggression displayed by particular breeds. This has been widely achieved, as demonstrated by the English Bulldog. Its ancestors had a very feisty and combative nature, according to contemporary accounts from the 1800s, whereas today these are very amenable animals, both toward people and other dogs. Increasingly, with dogs being kept primarily as pets, lack of aggression is a vital character trait. In some parts of the world, though, dogs, and especially strays, must still be approached with caution. They may be afflicted with rabies, causing them to become highly aggressive and dangerous.

Combat rituals

Dogs go through a number of stylized rituals before they actually attack, but this happens quickly and it is possible to miss the warning signs as the dog draws back its lips progressively to reveal its teeth. The sound of its growling becomes increasingly intense at the same time, combining a visual and vocal warning of its aggressive intent. This process is designed to intimidate, rather than attack, and the aggression will cease if the other dog withdraws. The aggressor is then simply likely to chase it for a short distance, with no physical harm resulting, providing that the other dog can run away easily. However, if it stands its ground, then the two dogs will fight. Bear in mind that puppies are not aggressive, and careful socialization and training, combined with neutering, should ensure that this state of affairs continues as they grow older.

Possessive behavior

Although it is often assumed that large dogs are the most aggressive, small dogs can also display similar behavior. They should not be underestimated, because they can cause painful injuries if they do bite. Rather than territorial aggression, though, many small dogs will display possessive behavior. This often relates to a favorite toy that the dog does not want to give up. It is very important to train your pet as a puppy to drop items on command and allow you to open its mouth without being aggressive (see page 33), to avoid such problems later in life.

False pregnancy

This is a very specific condition seen in unspayed bitches about eight weeks after their last season. It begins with a change in the bitch's behavior, causing her to become restless and seemingly devoted to a particular toy, which she will carry around with her. If you try to take this away, there is a real risk that she will become aggressive and you will be bitten. Hormonal changes may have led to her developing signs of pregnancy, such as swollen mammary glands, and even milk production. In the absence of any puppies, though, she will direct her maternal affection toward her toy and defend it at all costs.

TIP

- *Dogs may make a display of aggressive behavior with the aim of intimidation, rather than the intention to fight.*

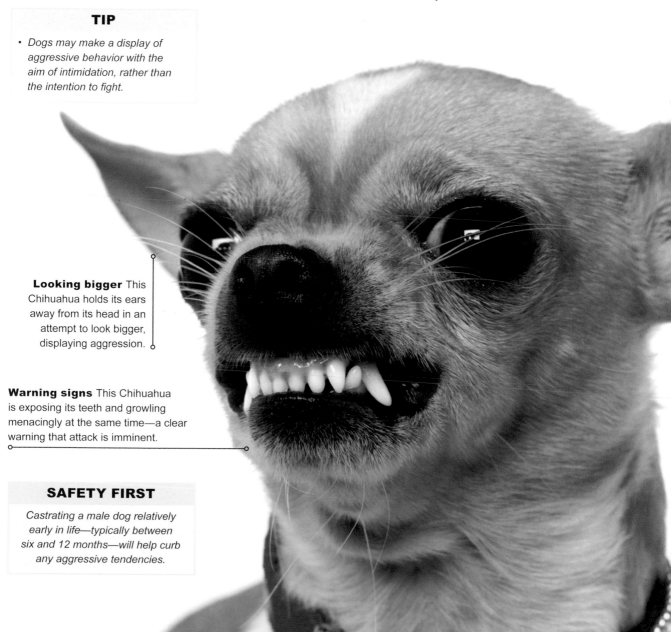

Looking bigger This Chihuahua holds its ears away from its head in an attempt to look bigger, displaying aggression.

Warning signs This Chihuahua is exposing its teeth and growling menacingly at the same time—a clear warning that attack is imminent.

SAFETY FIRST

Castrating a male dog relatively early in life—typically between six and 12 months—will help curb any aggressive tendencies.

Hostile meetings

Not every meeting between a dog and another of its kind will turn out to be a friendly encounter. You need to be especially careful if your dog has already clashed with a particular individual when on a walk. This hostility will not be forgotten if they meet again.

Renewing acquaintances

Dogs meeting for the first time tend to be more reserved than those that have previously encountered each other. In the latter case, the meeting may very quickly become aggressive. Alternatively, they may take little notice of one another, especially if they are relatively elderly. The dogs' reactions are likely to be influenced partly by their owners'; if they ignore each other and simply carry on walking in opposite directions, the dogs are likely to follow suit. However, if both owners stop and stand around talking, the dogs are more likely to start interacting with each other. They will sniff each other and may break into a game.

Enthusiastic approach This young dog is showing signs of enthusiasm toward the other, but they are not reciprocated. It will almost certainly withdraw rather than risk being bitten.

TIP

• Dogs are likely to be more short-tempered when the weather is thundery.

Snarl This dog is baring its teeth in a snarl in response to the dog advancing toward it.

Challenge This dog is challenging the other by opening its mouth and baring its teeth.

Angry response The teeth are very clearly exposed here, and just a short distance from the other dog's muzzle—very threatening behavior.

Possible explanation This dog may have been badly bitten by another when out for a walk. In this case it will be instinctively nervous and possibly aggressive in the company of other dogs for a while. You may need to consult a canine behaviorist for help.

TIP
- *Some dogs react aggressively even if there is no apparent threat.*

Avoiding trouble

If a dog is in any pain and confronted by a lively individual wanting to play, this is one situation where it will send a very clear message that it does not wish to participate in a game. Instead, it is likely to sit rooted to the spot and will bare its teeth, growling loudly so there is no doubt about the message. It is important to be aware of this possible reaction, even if under normal circumstances your dog is usually very friendly and playful. Try to exercise your pet far away from where it is likely to be confronted by loose dogs roaming off the leash until it has had time to recover.

Likewise, if it has been attacked by another dog, your pet is likely to be nervous, so try to switch your walking routine to a new area. But do not be surprised if your dog is wary of dogs of similar appearance in the future.

Keeping dogs apart

Not all displays of aggression when dogs meet are the result of direct conflict. They may happen as a defensive reaction. This is most likely to occur when you are walking your dog on a leash and another dog comes bounding up to you. Your own dog may feel trapped under these circumstances, especially if you try to pull your pet away and the other dog follows. The best course of action is to walk off quickly with your dog, rather than standing still. The other dog will soon lose interest. Staying still suggests that you are not retreating, and this might trigger a more aggressive response from the other dog. When two dogs meet on the leash, it is better simply to keep them apart, as such encounters can be quite unpredictable.

Fighting

Even a brief skirmish between domestic dogs can be very alarming, if you happen to witness it—and it can result in serious injury to the dogs involved. Fighting may have various causes but, in every case, it occurs because neither of the dogs involved is prepared to back down in response to clear warning signs.

Biting back
Although this dog is smaller than the other, it is responding just as aggressively.

HEIGHT ADVANTAGE
Here, the dog on the right is trying to force the other dog over, down onto the ground, using its height advantage. The smaller dog might, however, be able to break away and escape, thus avoiding being badly bitten by the other larger dog.

Fighting instincts

Certain types of dogs are more combative than others, especially the Bull Terrier breeds. This is a reflection of the fact that they were originally bred for dogfighting purposes. Bitches, however, tend to be less aggressive than male dogs, as are puppies, although this is the stage at which they must be adequately trained to minimize their combative instincts.

In the case of male dogs, neutering can help reduce aggressive instincts by lowering production of the male hormone testosterone, and it can also make them easier to train. If you know that your dog is inclined to be aggressive toward other dogs, it is important to muzzle your pet. The muzzle can be worn when you are out walking.

It is also a good idea to seek advice from a dog behaviorist—the cost of which may be covered under some pet insurance policies—on a one-to-one basis, with a view to addressing this problem. The sooner you seek advice, even from your veterinarian, the easier it may be to resolve the issue.

Communication breakdown

Play fighting often takes place between adult dogs that know each other well. This enables the dogs to test each other's strength and thereby maintain a social hierarchy without resorting to actual aggression. However, there is clear evidence that breeds that most closely resemble the wolf in appearance, such as the Siberian Husky, are much better equipped to communicate visually than others, such as the French Bulldog, which have been highly modified and can only display a far more limited range of threatening behaviors. This lack of subtlety in communication might cause a play fight to turn into the real thing, with both sides misinterpreting each other's intentions.

Breaking up fights

Domestic dogs not used to living in groups may misread or ignore the body language of other dogs. This means that in some cases, a dog will fight with an individual that has indicated that it is in no way a threat. When out in a park, where your dog is likely to encounter a number of different dogs, be prepared to call your dog back to you if you think that there could be conflict. Always be alert and try to anticipate any potential disagreements before they happen. If a fight does break out, do not try to separate the dogs by hand, as you are likely to be bitten. Instead, use the leash like a lasso to loop around your dog's neck and drag it to safety.

SAFETY FIRST

After a fight, be aware that your dog will be very distressed and may resent any attempt to examine its injuries.

Unsociable
Terrier-type dogs are often aggressive with each other, as they are not particularly social.

Disadvantage This elderly Jack Russell Terrier is at a distinct disadvantage, being smaller and shorter than its younger rival.

Out on the street

Do not be surprised if even a well-trained young dog starts to misbehave when you go out for the first time together on the street. There are many distractions in this particular environment, most often in the form of unfamiliar noises and smells.

Keeping close

Your dog is likely to want to stray to investigate what is going on all around it, so it may attempt to pull on the leash more than it has done in the past. An extendable (and retractable) leash gives you the opportunity to keep your dog close to you in this type of situation—allowing you to direct it to walk in a straight line. You can allow it more freedom in parks or the countryside.

Effective restraint

A harness—as worn by this Beagle—provides a safer means of control than a collar, because it prevents pressure from being applied on the vertebral column if the dog tries to pull ahead.

SAFETY FIRST

Make sure your dog cannot unexpectedly stray into the street, where it could easily be hit by a vehicle.

First experiences

It is important to allow your dog to experience walking on the street—otherwise it is likely to remain nervous in these surroundings for life. Try to avoid busy main streets initially. Increase your pet's confidence and concentration gradually, building on the basic training. At first, it is likely to be hard to even persuade your dog to walk well to heel, let alone sit at the edge of the street waiting to be able to cross safely. Be patient and persistent, though, and you will eventually get to this stage. It is a matter of being positive and reassuring and consistent in your instructions, as with any other aspect of training. Keep a close eye on your dog's body language, because it may show signs of loss of confidence and uncertainty at times (see pages 90–91), and will need more reassurance. This is likely to be a particular issue for a small dog in a crowd, some of whom may not be looking where they are walking. By keeping your dog close to you, there is less risk that it will be stepped on and hurt under these circumstances.

Tied up If you absolutely must leave your dog on the street while you go into a store, tie its leash securely to a sturdy object. But try to avoid such a situation.

CLEAN-UP TIME

It is vital, and usually a legal requirement, to clean up after your pet on the street and to train your dog to stay while you do so. If you regularly take the same route, you may find that the dog chooses roughly the same spot every time. This acts as a territorial marker (see pages 106–107).

Making friends

Many people like dogs and, especially if you have a cute-looking young dog, it is almost inevitable that someone will want to stroke your pet at some stage. Although most people ask before doing so, be prepared for others who just go ahead and talk to you at the same time. It is a very good idea to let people do this while your dog is still a youngster, as it will become used to meeting strangers and being stroked by them. This will help overcome any nervousness it may have (see pages 88–89).

Be aware, though, that if you own a small dog and pick it up and hold it close to you, thus inviting passersby to make a fuss over your pet, it may be inclined to act aggressively if it feels at all threatened.

Rescue dog

Being out with a rescue dog is slightly different, because the likelihood is—to a greater or lesser extent—that it will be more nervous by nature, and may react aggressively if it feels trapped. You need to spend time getting to know your dog and its particular traits in order to anticipate how it may act. Do not encourage strangers in the street to make a fuss over your pet, especially if it is very busy and you are surrounded by people. Simply tell them that your pet is a rescue dog, and that he has a rather shy, nervous nature.

In the countryside

There are a number of potential dangers that can catch a dog unaware in the countryside, posed by the landscape itself and the creatures that live there. You need to anticipate dangers that your pet may not understand and ensure that it will respond promptly when called.

TIP
- *Wild animals can transmit rabies; the vaccination of dogs is mandatory in certain areas.*

Be aware

Young dogs are instinctively curious, and this can lead them into danger, especially in unfamiliar surroundings. Always keep your dog close to you, calling it back if necessary, and putting it back on the leash if you need to. Young dogs may not understand the danger of venturing too near a fast-flowing river or the edge of a cliff, especially if distracted by chasing a bird. In the winter, the risk of falling through the relatively thin ice covering a lake should not be overlooked, either. Some breeds are more at risk in particular circumstances than others; Retrievers, for example, are drawn to water, where conditions may be dangerous. Fields containing livestock can be hazardous for dogs, as well as the livestock animals themselves (see pages 122–123), and dogs should always be kept on a leash in such areas.

COUNTRY LIVING
Some breeds are better suited to living in rural areas than in cities, with Black and Tan Coonhounds thriving in this type of location where they can run freely. It is important to match your choice of dog to the type of environment that you can provide.

PRICKLY PROTECTION

Slow-moving animals like tortoises and porcupines are fascinating to dogs, but their natural body armor provides protection. Porcupines should be avoided by dog owners: the quills are very painful.

Chasing birds

Dogs can disturb ground-nesting birds, so keep to paths when walking through fields where birds are likely to be breeding. Small songbirds are unlikely to interest dogs, but if a dog flushes out pheasants or other game birds, it might chase after them for some distance. The risk of danger is greater if waterfowl are involved, because the dog may plunge after them into water, where there could be a strong current. Dogs are generally good swimmers and so should be able to reach the safety of the shore again. In this situation, call your dog to you repeatedly, to give it a focus so it knows which way to swim, because it may be quite disoriented.

Cautious but risky approach

A dog's instinctive response when confronted by an animal or object with which it is unfamiliar will be to stand back, extend its neck, and sniff cautiously. In this way, it can withdraw quickly if necessary, springing up on its hind legs and retreating, should it become frightened. It will also be looking intently at the creature in question. If not alarmed on first inspection, however, the dog will reach out with its front paws and approach more closely. It may even attempt to prod at the creature which, in the case of a venomous snake, could have serious repercussions. A bite on the nose is more serious than on a foot, simply because the venom will take effect more quickly there.

Reptile identification

If you live in an area where there are venomous reptiles—especially snakes—familiarize yourself with the different species, so that if your dog confronts one and is bitten, you will be able to identify it.

If you have a cell phone with a camera, then you may also be able to photograph the snake, ensuring that effective, prompt treatment can be given. It also allows you to phone ahead and alert the veterinarian, so that they can be prepared to deal with your dog as soon as you arrive.

Curious posture The dog's tail is raised, and its ears extend forward as it investigates the snake.

Livestock

Always keep your dog on its leash when it is likely to encounter livestock. The relationship between dogs and other animals can be unpredictable, and dog owners must be proactive in ensuring that their pets do not cause distress, injury, or even death to livestock.

The risk with sheep

Livestock such as sheep hold a peculiar fascination for herding dogs. Even though such dogs are now most often domestic pets, their working instincts mean that they are often eager to observe and mingle with sheep. However, this leads to the possibility that their predatory, wolflike instincts will take over, and they will attack the sheep. This is especially likely when there are two or three dogs roaming on their own together as a pack. The risk is greatest at lambing time, when there may be afterbirths in the field and young lambs, too. Once a dog has attacked in this way, it is very likely to do so again in the future.

Working in pairs Farmers often teach their herding dogs to respond to slightly different signals, so that if two are working together, this will avoid any confusion between them as to which one should respond.

Herding strategies
Collie-type dogs use eye contact to control sheep, ensuring that they do not break out of the flock and scatter. Other herding breeds, such as the Australian Heeler and Welsh Corgi, keep cattle on the move from behind the herd by nipping at their heels.

TIP

• *You can never be sure how your dog will react to livestock, so keep it under control at all times.*

WORKING SHEEPDOGS

Working dogs such as this Corgi have grown up around sheep and are completely different from breeds of the same type seen in the show ring. It is the working attributes of such dogs that matter to farmers, rather than their appearance.

Stampeding cattle

Dogs tend to pick up on the nervousness of livestock, though this may not be apparent to you. It is very important to keep your dog on a leash, around cattle especially, even though your dog may not attack them. This is because of the panic-stricken way they might react to a dog on the loose, especially if there are calves with their mothers. A dog will instinctively recognize the danger and run off, but the cattle may start to stampede toward you.

Averting the risk

It is worth remembering that people are killed every year by cattle. Young cattle tend to be most curious, especially if they have not seen a dog before, and they may then try to cluster around you. Providing that you keep moving steadily with your dog on the leash, there should be no serious cause for concern, although it may be better to try to prevent this situation from arising in the first place by taking a detour.

SAFETY FIRST

Dogs do sometimes eat sheep droppings when out and about. Try to prevent this because it can upset their digestive system.

Watch for riders

Dogs are not drawn so instinctively to horses, but if you meet a horse and rider unexpectedly on a narrow path, this can be a very dangerous situation for all concerned. Your dog may be scared and start barking, which will in turn upset the horse, to the extent that it may rear up, unseat its rider, and run off—so stay alert.

Dogs and other animals

The adaptable nature of dogs is evident from the various stories that crop up from time to time—about associations with animals that would usually be quarry, for example. However, these incidents are very much the exceptions to the rule, and often there is no hope of the species getting along.

Stressful existence

The hunting instincts of domestic dogs have been developed over thousands of years. Hounds and other hunting breeds are therefore very likely to be instinctively drawn to a pet rabbit running up and down its run in the backyard. It is important to remember that although you may make the run absolutely dog-proof, the dog's presence can be very stressful as far as the rabbit is concerned, especially if it has nowhere to escape out of sight. In the wild, a rabbit would naturally bolt down its hole.

Dangers for dogs

Dogs, too, may encounter animals that could endanger their health. Getting too close to a porcupine, for instance, may result in painful pricks from its quills. It could also acquire porcupine fleas, which infest these animals on a temporary basis. Depending on where you live, your dog might also be at risk from venomous snakes.

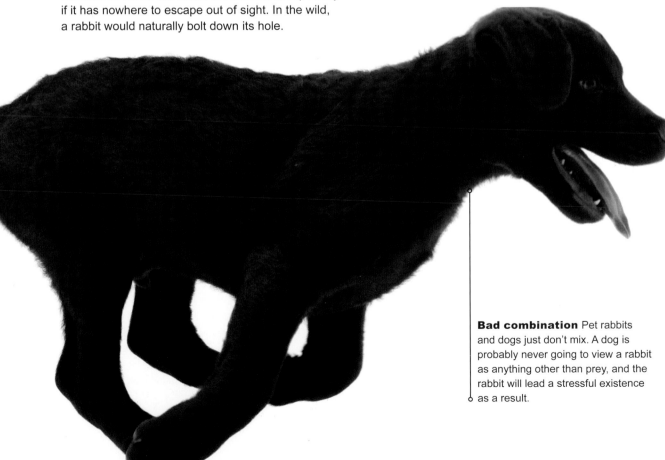

Bad combination Pet rabbits and dogs just don't mix. A dog is probably never going to view a rabbit as anything other than prey, and the rabbit will lead a stressful existence as a result.

Being friendly This young puppy is simply being curious and sniffing at the young kitten, lowering its head as a greeting, so they are touching noses.

Unhappy The fur on the kitten's tail and back is raised. These actions are intended to make it look bigger and more challenging, disguising the fact that it is petrified.

Gentle giant Although this Spinone Italiano pup is being friendly to the Siamese kitten—displaying no signs of aggression in its body language—its size is clearly intimidating.

Burrowing into trouble

When out for a walk, dogs may chase other animals, such as squirrels and even larger birds, when they are on the ground. The dog may not necessarily be displaying a strong hunting inclination in this situation, but simply looking for a reaction. As the bird will always take off and fly away, the dog will regard this as a game. Be especially careful when exercising Terriers, though, because of their tendency to "go to earth," disappearing into underground burrows that may have been dug by a host of creatures ranging from rabbits to rodents. If your dog is slightly overweight, there is a risk that it could become stuck underground. A few Terriers have managed to survive for at least ten days when stuck in a burrow or tunnel, and rescue services and animal welfare groups working together may be able to rescue dogs trapped in this way—however, it is better to avoid them getting stuck in the first place by being vigilant. Young Terriers are most at risk, with their innate curiosity combined with little sense of danger.

Out in front, for now The rabbit may be able to run away, this time. But do consider whether it could ever be happy sharing its space with a dog.

Digging

Many dogs display a strong desire to dig, especially Terriers, although other breeds also exhibit this behavior. Young dogs are most likely to behave in this way and may dig surprisingly fast at times, especially if they are in hunting mode.

Digging conditions

Dogs dig for a variety of reasons, sometimes simply to distract them from what they were doing before. This is what is known as "displacement activity." Young dogs are especially prone to digging, although ground conditions need to be favorable, and they will do so more readily in sand compared with hard clay or chalk. They will also prefer—often maddeningly from a gardener's perspective—to dig in a newly planted flowerbed rather than a fallow area of ground, simply because it is easier.

Backyard trouble

Digging is often linked to boredom, especially in the case of a young dog left outside in a backyard for any length of time. There may be scents there, too, that appeal to your dog—perhaps the addition of manure or bonemeal to your border. All you can do in this case is temporarily fence off the area. If you are planting bulbs, you do not want your dog digging these up and eating them, as they are toxic.

Head first This Border Collie is using its front paws to dig quickly through soft sand. Sand is a preferred digging medium, since it is relatively easy to displace. The dog's claws may help break up the ground when it starts digging.

Digging strategy

The body language of a dog when it is digging is generally one of excitement as it searches for something. Should you have two dogs together, either one or both may start digging in the same area, but they will be working independently rather than collaboratively. A dog may not just dig down through dirt, though—it may tunnel down through snow to reclaim a toy that has been buried or seek out bird food dropped from a feeder.

SAFETY FIRST

Dogs will sometimes enlarge the entrance to an animal burrow by digging and may risk falling in and becoming trapped underground.

Tail talk The tail is raised, confirming that the dog is alert and excited by digging. The hind legs provide support and anchorage, rather than being actively used as part of the digging process.

LEARNING BY EXAMPLE

Some dogs like to follow their owners' example—a dog tends not to dig like this if it is walking on a lead. Dogs enjoy digging on the beach, where the sand is soft and they can detect buried shellfish. They rarely eat these, however, instead simply sniffing at the shells after unearthing them.

Motivations for digging

Dogs rely on their front feet for digging—bending down slightly at first and scrabbling in the soil, effectively scraping it back as they do so. A dog may move around the perimeter of the hole as it digs, enlarging it from all sides. Throughout this process, which can entail some quite feverish digging, the dog retains a very alert expression, hoping to spot whatever it is searching for in the burrow. If this is a rodent, the dog will simply stop tunneling and give chase when the creature breaks cover.

On the other hand, there are times when dogs dig to bury objects. Bones are favored for this purpose, but toys may be treated in a similar way. This relates to the way in which wild dogs cache food by burying it, in the hope that it will be less likely to be detected and stolen by scavengers such as hyenas. This gives them the opportunity to return and feed again at a later time.

Odd friendships

The social nature of dogs means that they can sometimes forge unusual bonds with other animals in the domestic environment, as well as with other dogs. This is most likely to occur if you acquire a young puppy and cat at roughly the same time, so that they grow up together.

A kind of pack hierarchy

Dogs generally accept cats very readily, and in spite of the supposedly aloof nature of cats, a kitten will also strike up a friendship with a puppy. This may initially arise from the fact that both will seek out warm spots around the home to sleep and so may curl up together in front of a fire or next to a heater. Once they are roaming outside, the young dog will deter other cats from entering your backyard, thus protecting its feline companion from potential attack. In this way, the dog takes on a dominant role as pack leader, and the cat seems to recognize this.

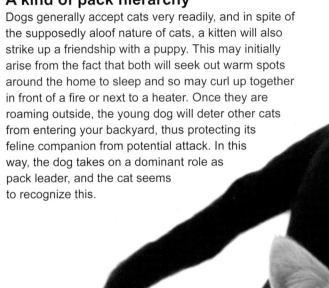

Building bonds

Kittens are actually more social than is generally recognized. If you obtain two littermates, they are likely to have a lifelong bond. In the absence of another cat, a kitten will happily pair up with a puppy.

TIP

- *Don't try to force a kitten and puppy to develop a relationship. It will evolve naturally over time.*

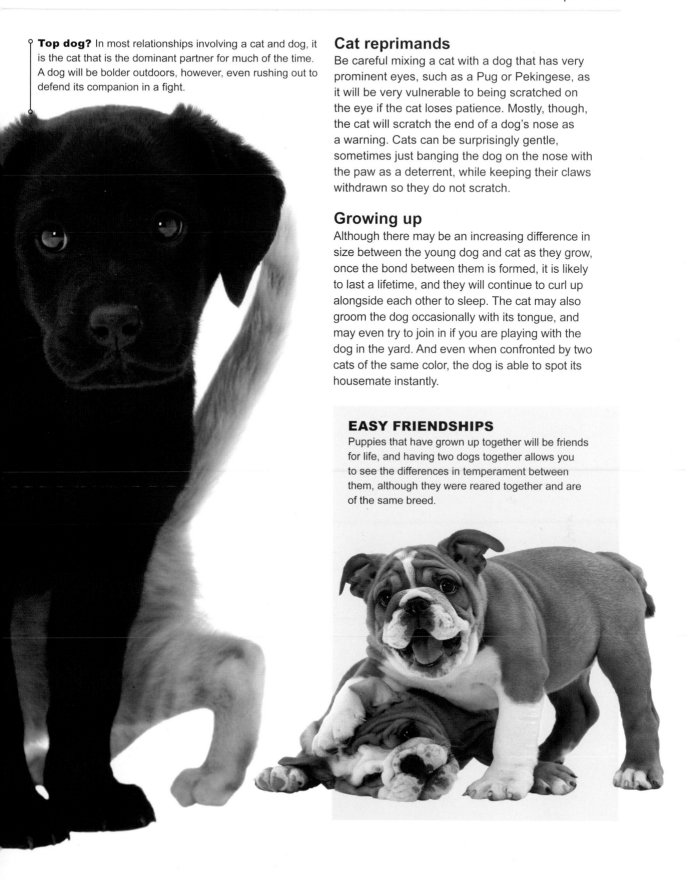

Top dog? In most relationships involving a cat and dog, it is the cat that is the dominant partner for much of the time. A dog will be bolder outdoors, however, even rushing out to defend its companion in a fight.

Cat reprimands

Be careful mixing a cat with a dog that has very prominent eyes, such as a Pug or Pekingese, as it will be very vulnerable to being scratched on the eye if the cat loses patience. Mostly, though, the cat will scratch the end of a dog's nose as a warning. Cats can be surprisingly gentle, sometimes just banging the dog on the nose with the paw as a deterrent, while keeping their claws withdrawn so they do not scratch.

Growing up

Although there may be an increasing difference in size between the young dog and cat as they grow, once the bond between them is formed, it is likely to last a lifetime, and they will continue to curl up alongside each other to sleep. The cat may also groom the dog occasionally with its tongue, and may even try to join in if you are playing with the dog in the yard. And even when confronted by two cats of the same color, the dog is able to spot its housemate instantly.

EASY FRIENDSHIPS

Puppies that have grown up together will be friends for life, and having two dogs together allows you to see the differences in temperament between them, although they were reared together and are of the same breed.

Lost dogs

Every year, a significant number of dogs stray from their owners and end up lost. This is most likely to happen in unfamiliar countryside and, thankfully, the majority are ultimately reunited, but this period of separation can be a worrying time for dogs and owners alike.

Wandering off

Young dogs love to explore and may wander off. Just because your dog responds well and returns readily when called during training sessions does not guarantee that it will react in this way when you are out together, especially if it is distracted by the sight of a rabbit or an interesting scent. Aim to prevent your dog from straying by continuing with its training when you are out in the countryside or park together. Use an extendable leash, which allows your dog to wander but prevents it from running off.

Staying in touch To avoid your dog getting lost, use an ultrasound whistle, set at a pitch that carries over a long distance. This will help your dog find its way back to you, especially if you blow it in a set pattern that the dog recognizes.

Going missing Even around the home, you may "lose" your dog. This Labrador Retriever has climbed into a box—a favorite pastime for many dogs.

On the trail

Certain types of dogs are more likely to run off than others—notably hounds, which will instinctively take off after a scent or if they see potential quarry, ignoring your entreaties to return. In this type of situation, stand your ground, rather than chasing after your pet, as it will simply see this as part of a game. The chances are, too, that your dog will outrun you.

Calling your dog back

By staying where you are, you can call your dog back to you. It will probably lose interest in the chase before long but then may be disorientated, especially in unfamiliar surroundings. Your calls will help your dog find you again. Always praise it when it returns, rather than scolding it, to make this a positive learning experience for your pet. If possible, try to avoid exercising a young dog off the leash at dusk, because if it does disappear, it will be much harder for you to find your pet as darkness falls.

Microchipping

The earlier you notice that your dog is missing, the better your chances of finding your pet. The best chance of you being reunited will be if your dog is microchipped with a unique marker. The number of the chip will be held in a central database accessible to animal rescue agencies and other groups dealing with strays, and there are some remarkable stories of dogs being found in this way months—and even occasionally years—after they disappeared.

Finding its way home

Provided that your dog can avoid the hazard of passing traffic and has not actually been stolen, it will ultimately come into contact with people. It might be seen hanging around a street or may start following someone else home in your absence. Its ability to return to your home will depend to some extent on how far away it was when it became lost. In addition, it also depends on how familiar your dog is with the local area, as to whether it can use sights and scents to navigate back. Neutering will usually suppress a dog's urge to roam in the first place, which is a good reason for your dog having this surgical procedure.

STRAY DOGS

In most major cities there are some dogs, sadly, that spend much of their time on the streets, even being born there. Their lives are much shorter than those of pet dogs, with each day bringing a constant struggle for survival, especially in terms of finding food.

Scavenging Dogs that have strayed will need to find food, and they can often be seen scavenging. Unlike their wild relatives, domestic dogs are unlikely to hunt for their food in this situation. Consequently they may end up eating rotten or even dangerous food items, making themselves sick.

SAFETY FIRST

Be certain that your backyard is secure, with no gaps under fences that will allow your dog to escape from the property.

Special Skills

All kinds of dogs with special attributes

Guard
dogs

Water
dogs

Retrievers

Drug
detection

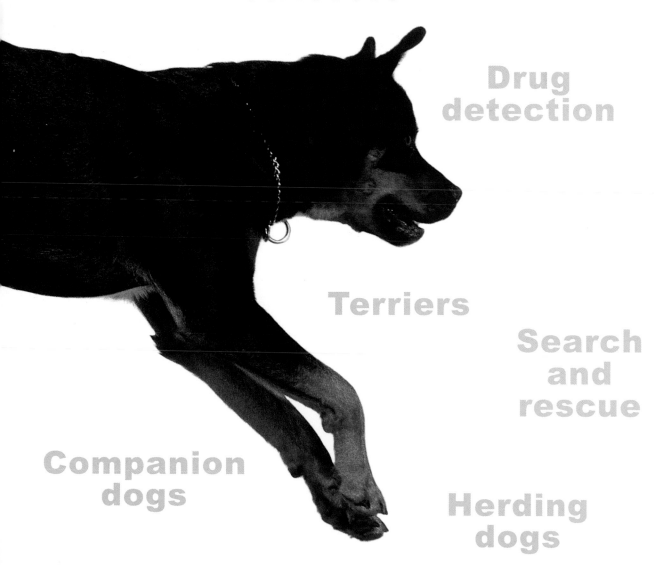

Terriers

Search
and
rescue

Companion
dogs

Herding
dogs

133

How dogs differ

It is remarkable that all of today's domestic dogs, in their many forms and colors, are descended from the Gray Wolf. Many breeds were evolved for particular tasks, and this has helped shape their typical appearance and behavior.

Great variety

The most obvious point of variance between breeds is in terms of size. This ranges from the tiny Chihuahua, standing barely 6 in. (15 cm) tall at the shoulder, up to the Great Dane, which can be more than 36 in. (91 cm) in height. Size has an impact on the life expectancy of the different breeds—the giant breeds have a much shorter life expectancy than members of the toy group.

Another distinguishing feature is coloration, with a few breeds being defined in part by this characteristic, as with the Black Russian Terrier, for example. In other cases, the breed encompasses several recognized colors or patterns. Allied to coloration, of course, is coat type and length. Shorthaired dogs, perhaps unsurprisingly, tend to originate from warmer parts of the world, whereas longhaired dogs generally come from colder parts of the world.

The actual build of the dog is quite variable, too, and is influenced by its function. For instance, breeds bred to run fast, such as the Greyhound, have relatively long bodies, helping maximize the amount of ground they can cover in a single stride.

SAFETY FIRST

Always research the background of a breed that appeals to you in order to gain an insight into its character.

Shorthaired breed
In Mediterranean hounds, such as this Pharaoh Hound from Malta, the absence of a thick, insulating undercoat means that the fur lies flat against the body.

Muzzle shape This hound's muzzle is relatively long, whereas a number of breeds, such as the Pekingese, have a decidedly compact facial appearance. This can not only compromise their ability to control their body temperature, but may also result in overcrowding of teeth in the mouth.

TIP

• *Working breeds tend to be very energetic and need a lot of exercise.*

Tough worker The Australian Cattle Dog is well suited to working in the harsh Australian landscape. The development of many working breeds has been similarly influenced by their environment.

Extraordinary longevity

The Australian Cattle Dog (left) has now built up a worldwide following, having been bred originally for herding cattle. It needed to be a tough breed, able to survive in the hot, arid Australian Outback, and wild Dingoes were used to contribute to its development (see pages 42–43). Today, this breed holds the record for longevity for domestic dogs. An individual named Bluey, kept in Australia, lived for more than 29 years— more than twice as long as the majority of dogs.

Puffin hunter

One of the most specialized of all domestic dog breeds is the rare Norwegian Lundehund—also known as the Norwegian Puffin Dog. These dogs were used to hunt puffins—seabirds that nest in burrows on the sheer cliff faces in Norway—a popular source of food among local people. The dogs display the phenomenon of polydactylism, having extra toes that are similar to our thumbs, helping the dog maintain its grip on sheer cliffs more effectively. Its neck is also very flexible, and their front legs can twist around. These traits combine to make the Lundehund an expert puffin hunter.

Hairless dogs

Among the most unusual types of dogs are the various hairless breeds. These originate in the main from parts of Central and South America, where they were kept by the Incas and other nearby cultures, serving as bed warmers, companions, and also food sources on occasions. The best-known example of this group today is the Mexican Hairless Dog, or Xoloitzcuintle.

Outside of the New World, the only other hairless breed is the Chinese Crested Dog. As might be expected, these dogs are vulnerable to the cold, and those with pink skin are susceptible to sunburn. They can also be rather prone to obesity, thanks to their large appetites, and it is not uncommon for them to lack some teeth. It is believed that there also used to be similar breeds kept by tribes in North America, but these are now extinct.

Hardly any hair
This Mexican Hairless Dog does in fact have some scant hair on the extremities of its body.

Specialist breeds

As well as the more familiar breeds, there is quite an array of more unusual dogs, adapted to their particular environment and the tasks they are expected to perform. Some have remained unchanged for thousands of years.

Distinctive calls

The island of New Guinea, north of Australia, is home to an especially unusual type of feral dog, which lives in a semidomesticated state. The New Guinea Singing Dog is best known for its distinctive calls, which have been compared to yodeling. Once one dog starts calling, other members of the group join in. They can change the pitch of their howl very effectively and are also mimics—in the company of dogs that bark, they will start to do so, too.

Unusual behavior

There are some very distinctive behaviors unique to New Guinea Singing Dogs, such as the way they toss their heads quickly to the side when seeking attention, that seem to confirm that they have long been isolated. They live in a semiwild state, and studies suggest that they are less pack-oriented than wolves. Rather aggressive by nature toward others of their own kind, they are very effective hunters.

Another unusual trait is that the bitches tend to be dominant. They are also differentiated from true domestic dogs by the size of their carnassial teeth, used to slice meat into chunks that can be swallowed easily. These are significantly larger, a characteristic also associated with wild canids. Although no longer as common as they were on New Guinea, they do still survive there. A number are now also kept in the U.S. and elsewhere in the world.

Relationships DNA studies suggest New Guinea Singing Dogs are closely related to Dingoes, and have probably been isolated from other ancestral lines for at least 5,000 years. In terms of domestic dogs, they are most closely allied to some of Asia's oldest breeds.

SAFETY FIRST

New Guinea Singing Dogs are so agile as to be almost catlike in the way that they climb and jump, so plan backyard fencing accordingly.

Old Japanese breed

The roles of dogs have changed significantly over time, often becoming more specialized, although many originally shared a background in hunting. The Japanese Akita is one of the breeds that shares common ancestral roots with the New Guinea Singing Dog. It was used as far back as the 1600s by the Shogun, Japan's ruling elite, to track bears on the island of Hokkaido. Akitas were also bred for dogfighting over subsequent centuries but, more recently, the breed's role has diversified. It has been kept as a guardian, seen service as a police dog, entered the show ring, and become popular as a companion breed worldwide.

Endangered working breeds

Specialized working breeds remain most at risk of becoming extinct, but one that has made a remarkable comeback over recent years has been the Portuguese Water Dog, which shares a common ancestry with the Standard Poodle. For centuries, it was used by fishermen off the Algarve coast, barking when it spotted schools of fish in the water and also to warn about collisions between boats in fog.

Famous breed In the 1960s, there were fewer than 50 Portuguese Water Dogs. Now they are far more numerous, with the breed achieving massive publicity thanks to Bo, selected as a pet by President Obama and his family.

HUNTING IN THE TREES

Coonhounds have some of the most unusual hunting habits of all dogs. These breeds, which have been developed in the U.S. and are rare elsewhere, often hunt raccoons, as indicated by their name. They chase raccoons up into the trees and stay at the bottom, barking and jumping up, which is why they are are also known as treeing dogs. This Coonhound (right) is being trained to behave in this fashion.

Companion dogs

Today, the majority of dogs are kept as companions, rather than for their original working purposes. In the past, however, only a relatively small number of breeds fulfilled this particular role. Many of those that survive today, such as the Italian Greyhound, were in fact originally "scaled-down" versions of bigger working dogs.

A long history

The keeping of companion dogs has always been linked with settled and reasonably affluent societies. Excavations of Roman sites in Europe have revealed the presence of such dogs, as have finds from ancient Mayan, Aztec, and Toltec settlements in Central America dating back more than 3,000 years. This trend continued, with such dogs becoming very popular among the royal courts of Europe during the Middle Ages.

One of the earliest surviving lineages is represented by the Bichon group of breeds. These dogs are believed to have originated in Italy, and from there were taken to other areas of the world. Very similar breeds exist today on islands as far away as Cuba—home of the Havanese, Tenerife, and Madagascar. The Maltese is also a member of this group. The appearance and behavior of these different breeds are very similar; they are known for being playful and adaptable animals.

SAFETY FIRST

Miniaturization has led to physical problems in companion breeds. They often suffer from patellar luxation, a weakness affecting the kneecaps.

Pampered pet The name Bichon is derived from the French word *bichonner*, meaning "to pamper." This description may have arisen because of Henry III of France (1551–1589). He kept a Bichon that was a particular favorite and always accompanied him on his royal journeys, traveling in a special basket.

Playful and quick to learn

Historically, companion dogs were kept simply for amusement and company. This has led to traits that set them apart from other types of dogs. These breeds, of which the Bichon Frisé is the most commonly kept example, tend to display playful temperaments. They instinctively want to interact with their owners and learn by example, developing a routine very quickly. This helps to explain why, after falling out of favor as royal companions in the 1800s, these dogs soon found themselves in demand as street performers, because they worked so well with their handlers.

Covered ears The ears are often covered in long hair and so are used less for communication purposes in the toy breeds.

Overdependent As a result of living alongside people, the focus of these dogs is very much on their owners, to the extent that they can develop behavioral problems. They may display signs of separation anxiety if their routine changes and will pine if left on their own for long periods.

Physically varied

Companion dogs are very diverse in appearance. The one characteristic that links them is their small size, which is why they are often described as "toy" breeds. They were not bred for a particular physical trait—only a friendly temperament—and stem from widely different ancestral lineages. These breeds communicate largely by close, direct contact with their owners. As a result, the ways in which toy dogs use body language is less marked than in other dogs. Their tails are relatively immobile, and are also often covered with hair, reducing flexibility.

Assistance dogs

The ability of dogs to work alongside people, coupled with their superior senses, has led to their use as companions to assist those with disabilities. Guide dogs are the best known example, but there are also dogs trained to help people with hearing impairments and even epilepsy.

The first guide dogs

Records exist of dogs being used to aid visually impaired people as far back as the 1550s, but the practice did not become widespread until the early 1900s. The first training schools for this purpose were set up in Germany, with the aim of helping soldiers who had been blinded in World War I. An American dog trainer named Dorothy Harrison Eustis witnessed these dogs working when she was in Europe and wrote an article about them when she returned home. This was published in 1927 under the title of *The Seeing Eye*. Morris Frank, a blind man from Nashville, Tennessee, then contacted her for help with training a dog that he could use.

Guide dogs today

Two years later, the first guide dog school opened in the U.S. and took its name directly from the title of Eustis' article. The Seeing Eye relocated in 1931 from Tennessee to Morristown, New Jersey, where it still has its headquarters today. Three years later, the U.K.'s Guide Dogs for the Blind Association was founded. That organization now runs four training schools as well as operating a National Breeding Center, raising more than 1,100 puppies annually, and is supported by a nationwide volunteer network.

TIP

- *All assistance dogs must have a friendly, intelligent, and docile nature.*

SAFETY FIRST

Dogs are partially color-blind so they cannot help people across the road based on the color of the traffic lights.

Ideally suited Retrievers are hugely popular as assistance dogs. However, they are not great for people who are allergic to dogs; for this purpose, the Labradoodle was developed (see page 160).

TAKING THE LEAD

A guide dog is able to help its handler move around obstacles and avoid stepping out onto the street, but it is not able to tell where the person wants to go, and so requires direction. In other cases, though, with seizure-alert dogs, for example, they will take the initiative. A trained dog of this type may be able to indicate to its handler that an epileptic attack is likely, before this actually occurs.

All shapes and sizes

In the early days, German Shepherds were most commonly used, including Morris Frank's first dog, named Buddy. The list of breeds trained for this purpose has since expanded significantly, with Golden Retrievers and Labrador Retrievers frequently chosen. Other breeds have proved to be suitable, too, ranging from Yorkshire Terriers and Papillons to Dobermans and Rottweilers.

Hearing dogs

Hearing dogs are there to alert those with impaired hearing to critical everyday sounds, such as a smoke alarm going off or a doorbell ringing. They may also help outside the home and can usually be identified by their bright orange collars. Lively crossbreeds are generally chosen for this purpose, between six and 12 months of age, and often obtained from local animal shelters. The dog indicates a sound by touching the person and then goes toward its source.

Starting out
Socialization for would-be assistance dogs is incredibly thorough. Puppies live in foster homes at first, with serious training not starting until they are at least one year old.

TIP

• The terms "service dog" and "assistance dog" are often used interchangeably.

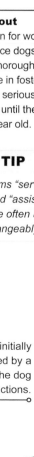

Long training Training initially teaches the key skills, followed by a period of up to a year when the dog learns to ignore distractions.

Guard dogs

It is easy to understand how dogs became valued as guardians around settlements, especially at night. Their superior senses make them much better suited than humans to the detection of danger, due not only to their acute hearing but also their sharp eyesight.

Communication is key

Although guard dogs are often regarded as aggressive, this should not be the case. Well-trained dogs of this type are very responsive to the commands of their handler, working alongside them in the same way that members of a wolf pack operate together when out hunting. A poorly trained guard dog is a distinct liability, though, and is likely to turn on a friend as soon as a foe. Certain breeds are commonly chosen as guard dogs, notably the German Shepherd and, to a lesser extent, the Rottweiler and Doberman. These dogs tend to be used because they are intelligent and responsive, having evolved to work closely with people.

Adaptable dog German Shepherds will respond to vocal commands, but are also adept at interpreting hand signals and so are able to work silently. Their natural intelligence has led to them being widely employed. They work as guide dogs, with the police and the army, and are also popular companions.

TIP

- *Guard dogs can make good pets, but training is essential with these large breeds.*

Excellent hearing Guard dogs can detect the slightest sounds of a possible intruder.

Barking encouraged

One area where a significant difference has developed between wolves and their domestic relatives—especially guard dogs—is in the way that they vocalize. Whereas wolves are quiet, guard dogs are often actively encouraged to bark to alert their owners to a possible threat. This is also an effective means of intimidating an intruder.

Hunter turned protector

Perhaps the most remarkable turnaround in canine behavior is the way in which domestic dogs have been used to protect sheep and other livestock from being preyed on by wolves. Reared in close proximity to a flock over generations, a dog transfers its loyalty to its new pack leader—the shepherd—in much the same way that dogs do to their owners when they become household pets.

Flock-guardian breeds include the Kuvasz, whose origins are in the area of modern-day Hungary; the Maremma Sheepdog, developed in central Italy; and the Great Pyrenees, from the border area between France and Spain. Another example is the Polish Tatra Sheepdog.

Instincts remain The temperament of pet guard dogs still reflects their working origins. Alert and loyal by nature, they bark readily if they detect danger.

SEEING IN THE DARK

A dog's ability to see in relative darkness reflects the nocturnal habits of wolves. They retain a high percentage of the cells (rods) on the retina at the back of the eye where the image forms. This means that they can see well at night. However, their color vision is not as acute.

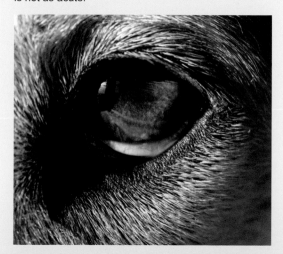

Blending in One of the significant features of flock guardians such as this Greet Pyrenees is that they are predominantly white in color, enabling them to merge very effectively with the flocks of sheep that they protect.

Herding dogs

The ability of dogs to work with sheep—and other types of domestic livestock, from reindeer to chickens—is unique. This skill relies on harnessing some of the hunting instincts of the gray wolf but using them in a way that does not cause harm to the animals.

Working closely

Training a dog for herding tasks relies on a very close understanding between dog and handler from an early age. It is a very different process from obedience training, which takes place primarily at close quarters.

The sharp eyesight of herding dogs is very important, as it enables them to follow hand signals that are frequently given from some distance away. Herding dogs also have sharp hearing and learn to follow voice commands as well. Flexibility is key to the interactions between handler and herding dog, as, for example, they need to deal with unexpected situations such as a sheep suddenly breaking away from a small group.

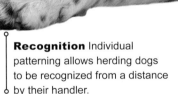

Recognition Individual patterning allows herding dogs to be recognized from a distance by their handler.

In the eyes

Herding dogs do not only use their eyes to follow their handler's instructions but also as a means of controlling the livestock. This is similar to the way in which a wolf focuses on its quarry. Remarkably, sheep will recognize this stare and will react to the dog as if it were a wolf (though they won't ultimately be attacked by it).

Studies suggest that some breeds of dogs are naturally more talented herders than others, but there is also a learned component, with young herding dogs needing to be taught. They can learn both from their trainer and from watching other dogs at work.

Herding dogs, unlike flock guardians can be very noisy, as they will use their ability to bark as a way of helping to control the movements of the livestock. Their tails are less significant in terms of communicating, however, and in fact litters born to many herding breeds contain bobtails—individuals that naturally have short tails.

THE MERLE GENE

The merle gene is responsible for the so-called "blue" appearance seen in the coat of some herding breeds, such as Rough and Smooth Collies and the Cardigan Corgi, but it can have unfortunate side effects. If two merles are mated together, this will increase the likelihood of the puppies being deaf or afflicted by sight problems. Deaf dogs appear unresponsive, although veterinary tests will be needed to confirm this disability.

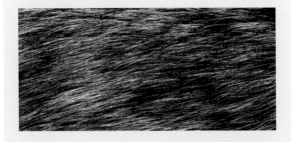

COMPETITIONS

Although bred to work with livestock, the adaptable nature of herding dogs means they can excel in other areas, such as obedience and agility competitions, as well as heel work to music—effectively a type of dance competition.

Friendly nature Herding dogs' close relationship with people means that they are instinctively friendly, and do not make especially good watchdogs, unlike flock guardians (see page 143).

Sharp eyes Eyesight is the sharpest sense in herding dogs compared to any other group. Unfortunately, they also suffer from more genetic problems in this regard, and breeding stock should be screened accordingly.

Ear carriage The ears of herding dogs are quite variable in appearance. They may hang forward, as here—"drop-eared"— or be erect.

Adapting to the home

The appeal of a well-trained herding dog is unmistakable, but unfortunately this is not the whole story. It is easy to assume that dogs that form such a close bond with people make ideal household pets. But there can very easily be a communication breakdown in the home environment.

The problem is that although herding dogs will instinctively develop a rapport with their owners, they would normally spend much of their day outdoors. Working (as distinct from show) bloodlines, in particular, will not settle well if they are cooped up in the home for long periods every day.

Herding dogs will become bored and frustrated if this happens, and this can cause them to become destructive, especially if they are left alone for any length of time. Whereas young puppies of any breed are likely to cause some damage at around six months of age (when they are teething), this problem will likely persist in the case of herding dogs, if their living conditions are unsuitable. If you have other pets, such as chickens, it is also not uncommon for a herding dog to start to try to round them up if they are roaming free.

Terriers

Not all small dogs are lap dogs; Terriers, for example, are a very energetic group due to their working origins. The majority of today's Terrier breeds originated in the British Isles. The biggest is the Airedale Terrier, which stands 23 in. (58 cm) high at the shoulder.

Terrier characteristics

The name "Terrier" comes from the Latin word *terre*, meaning "earth," and reflects the fact that one of the main tasks of these lively dogs was to venture into the underground lairs of a variety of animals, including foxes and badgers. This called for a brave, determined, and bold nature that is still evident in such breeds today.

   With certain notable exceptions, such as the West Highland White, affectionately known as the Westie, many Terrier breeds are now in serious decline today. Terriers are dogs with strong links to the past agricultural heritage of the British Isles, and are independent animals with high energy levels. They have tended not to be as popular among owners seeking a small dog, compared with the true companion breeds, which are less feisty. The grooming needs of many Terriers are also quite demanding, which makes them more difficult to prepare for the show ring than some breeds. Changing fashions have also played a part in the decline of breeds such as the Wire-coated Fox Terrier.

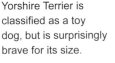

Feisty The tiny Yorkshire Terrier is classified as a toy dog, but is surprisingly brave for its size.

Versatile companions

As working dogs, Terriers are far more versatile than their origins may suggest. These breeds evolved largely in rural areas and, although not household pets as such, they were a common sight on farms. They would help to control vermin such as rats, as well as acting as guardians, with their loud barking serving to alert farm workers to the approach of visitors. This trait is still very apparent in Terriers today, which are more reliant on vocal communication than most other groups of dogs.

SAFETY FIRST

Many Terriers still display a tendency to bark persistently, often to attract attention, and should be trained not to do so.

Built for digging A relatively long body, short legs, and powerful hindquarters enable a Terrier to move easily underground. These characteristics typify the so-called "earth breeds" of Terrier, such as this Jack Russell, one of the most popular members of the group.

Characteristic ears

The increased emphasis on vocalization in Terriers may be linked to their appearance—the ears of many breeds are relatively small and folded down along the sides of their heads, and so cannot be used for a range of communication as in some other breeds. They protect this vulnerable part of the body from injury and also help prevent loose soil from entering the ears when the dog is underground. Terriers readily move their ears forward, however, to indicate interest. When out for a walk, this signal indicates that they have detected quarry, such as a rat.

Fighting origins

Many members of the group are noted for scrapping with each other, and some of the bigger breeds, such as the Staffordshire Bull Terrier, were actually created for fighting purposes. This trend has continued with the more recent development of the notorious American Pit Bull Terrier, which has been banned in many countries because of its aggression, toward other dogs, and even humans.

Powerful build
English Bull Terriers are strong, well-muscled dogs, reflecting their lineage as Terriers originally bred for fighting purposes.

What to expect

The active nature of Terriers means that they are less suitable than true companion breeds as pets, especially in urban areas. Socialization from an early age is very important as a means of ensuring that they are not aggressive toward other dogs. Terriers also often display a strong tendency to dig, sometimes simply in flower beds, although occasionally a Terrier may be able to tunnel out under the garden fence and escape into the street. Their desire to "go to earth" is a lasting reflection of their working ancestry.

Many breeds are generally less responsive to training than other small dogs, having evolved over the course of centuries on farms, where they roamed by themselves. However, there is no doubting the appealing character of Terriers. While training may be more difficult, they are always ready to play, whether chasing after a ball or testing their strength with a tug toy. These are small dogs with big hearts and plenty of energy.

Watchdog Terriers like this Airedale are always alert, which means they make excellent watch dogs.

Pointers

Dogs have always had an important role as hunting companions, helping their owners procure food. Sporting dogs (or gun dogs) can be divided into the Setters and Pointers (shown here) and the Retrievers and Spaniels (pages 150–151).

Pointers

Another group of dogs of ancient lineage, Pointers had already developed as a known type by the 1600s. Their origins date back to the Middle Ages, with the Spanish Pointer being the ancestral breed. These sporting companions became increasingly refined in appearance, although their physique has also been shaped by the type of terrain in which they work. Many breeds of pointer, such as the Old Danish Pointer, still remain localized today. This is a highly adaptable breed, with good tracking skills as well as excellent retrieving abilities.

Built for sniffing out quarry The wide nostrils of this Pointer reveal its scenting abilities. Even pet Pointers will instinctively adopt the characteristic pointing stance when they detect potential quarry, without any special training.

Different skills Although Pointers are adept at locating game, they are less well suited to retrieving it and are not eager to venture into water. This led to the development of a different type of dog—the Retriever.

Setters

The setter group, whose name derives from the old English word *set*—meaning "to sit"—indicate game in their vicinity by sitting down, or sometimes even lying down. This gives the accompanying huntsman a clear line of fire at the target.

The most popular of the setter breeds over recent years has been the Irish Setter, sometimes incorrectly called the Red Setter because of its striking coloration. It typifies the lively and rather wayward temperament of such dogs, tending to run off quite readily whenever an interesting scent presents itself.

Thick coat Irish Setters need frequent brushing to keep their coats free from tangles. The coat is thicker in winter.

Distinctive pose A Pointer will indicate the presence of game by adopting an unmistakable "pointing" posture. The dog stands with its body still, head relatively low, and tail and neck extended.

SAFETY FIRST

Gun dogs often become muddy when being exercised in country areas. Simply wait for the mud to dry and then you can brush it out easily.

TIP

• *Pointers are relatively easy to train, being used to working closely with people on a one-to-one basis. They are affectionate by nature, and not especially noisy, in contrast to Spaniels, which can be excitable.*

Temperament matters By adopting this frozen stance, there is no risk of the Pointer alerting a hunted bird or animal to its presence.

Retrievers

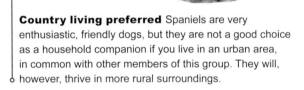

This sub-group of sporting dogs includes the Spaniels, bred to flush out game, and the Retrievers, bred to fetch it. The Labrador Retriever has become the most numerous breed in the world and is very popular as a family pet, due to its genial nature and good looks.

The need for the Retriever

Back in the 1800s, as the shooting of game with guns became fashionable as a leisure pursuit among the wealthy, so demand grew for a new type of dog. It would not need to detect the presence of game and flush it out, for which purposes Setters, Pointers, and Spaniels already existed, but rather, it would work alongside its handler to retrieve the birds after they had been shot. This would require both stamina and an obedient nature, as well as an ability to adapt, in terms of its working behavior.

Country living preferred Spaniels are very enthusiastic, friendly dogs, but they are not a good choice as a household companion if you live in an urban area, in common with other members of this group. They will, however, thrive in more rural surroundings.

Changing roles

The working role of members of the Retriever group has diversified markedly from just being sporting companions, as they adapted to being employed for many more useful tasks in society during the 20th century. Yet the same basic skills learned as gun dogs have made them suitable for other work. The noise of guns firing, for example, is not dissimilar to the sound of traffic on a busy street. As a consequence, traffic noise does not deter Labrador Retrievers from being highly effective as guide dogs (see page 140).

Spaniels at work

Spaniels operate in a different manner from Setters or Pointers; they flush out game, often in wooded areas where there is plenty of cover. The thick, heavy, pendulous ear flaps of these dogs are relatively immobile and help protect the inner ears from injury when the dogs are working in thick undergrowth. Just as with Pointers, so the various breeds of Spaniels evolved to work in different types of terrain, adapting their working methods to that of their environment.

CROSSOVER DOG

Some Spaniels, usually used for flushing, work well as retrievers. One of the assets needed for this task is a sound temperament, as dogs with a nervous nature will be upset by the noise of the guns.

SAFETY FIRST

Kept as household pets, Labrador Retrievers can easily pile on the pounds as they grow older. Keep a regular check on your pet's weight as it ages.

Retriever developments

Just as happened with the previous generation of sporting dogs (Pointers), so Retrievers diversified, with specific breeds being developed for different terrains. In a few cases, as with the Hungarian Vizsla, which was developed to work on the plains of Hungary, what had been a Pointer morphed into a dual-purpose Pointer and Retriever. But the key difference between these two breed sub-groups can be found by delving into their respective ancestries. Unlike Pointers, the majority of Retrievers were bred from stock that was used to working in or around water. Labradors, for example, were descended from what was known as the St. John's Dog in its native Newfoundland, where it used to assist fishermen hauling in their nets. These working dogs contributed not just to the development of the Labrador, but also both the flat-coated and curly-coated Retrievers. Meanwhile, in North America itself, dedicated gun dogs such as the Chesapeake Bay Retriever and the Nova Scotia Duck-tolling Retriever came into being. The latter breed aided the waiting hunters at the outset, by splashing around in the water as a way of attracting or "tolling" waterfowl within range of their guns.

Spot the difference The Golden Retriever has a noticeably longer, wavier coat than the Labrador Retriever. Golden Retrievers are only bred in one color, but this can vary in depth.

Good companions?

Members of the gun dog group have evolved to work in particular habitats, with many being quite specialized. They all establish a strong rapport with their handler, but it is the Spaniels, which are the smallest members of the group and therefore best suited to domestic surroundings, that are now most widely kept as pets. Although they are very enthusiastic and friendly by nature, these dogs are full of energy and need to be given plenty of opportunity to exercise in order to be happy.

Differing appearance There is now a distinct divergence in the appearance of popular gun dogs—such as Golden Retrievers, for instance—depending on whether they are bred for show purposes or as working gun dogs. Working dogs tend to have a rangier and less uniform type, being judged at field trial events essentially on their abilities rather than their appearance.

Sighthounds

The hounds are regarded as the oldest domesticated dogs. Representations of dogs similar to Greyhounds existed in Ancient Egypt, 6,000 years ago. The hounds have been divided into a group that hunt mainly by scent (see pages 154–155), while others track their quarry by sight.

Bred for heat

Many sighthounds were originally bred in hot, arid climates—on the fringes of the Sahara Desert, for example. This means that they have short, fine-textured coats, with no dense, insulating undercoat. As a result, they are prone to feeling the cold in more northerly latitudes and should wear coats when being exercised over the winter months.

Fit for purpose

The appearance of the head of a typical sighthound, if viewed from the front, has been likened to an upside-down pear. Sighthounds have (as their name would suggest) excellent eyesight for detecting distant movement, which could indicate a prey species such as a gazelle. Their facial shape means that their eyes are located in a forward position, at the front of the face rather than on the sides. This enables them to focus more effectively and to judge distance, with the nasal area being elongated and quite narrow. The narrow nasal passages help the dog stay cool, but are less well equipped to pick up scents, compared with a scenthound (see pages 154–155). Working on their own to detect and chase prey, sighthounds display rapid acceleration, with Greyhounds being able to reach a top speed of 45 mph (70 km/h) over short distances.

Working in pairs Sighthounds normally hunt singly, but in Russia it was traditional for Borzois to hunt in pairs, pursuing wolves. They needed to overpower the wolf and hold it down until the huntsmen caught up and killed it with a sword or dagger.

Stealth attack

Sighthounds are sprinters, not long-distance runners. Success depends on getting the hound as close as possible to its target while retaining the element of surprise. In North Africa, native sighthounds are therefore traditionally carried by riders on camels, with hawks being used to harry the target ahead, before the sighthounds are released to run down their quarry.

Personality

Sighthounds tend to be rather shy, even nervous, dogs in the company of strangers, but are very relaxed with people they know well. They are gentle by nature and tend not to be boisterous or dominant, but are always alert. Their flattish ears, set well back on the sides of the head, can indicate excitement or interest by being held slightly away from the head in a more forward position.

The tail, which is long and rather narrow, extends down between the hind legs, often displaying a slight upward curve at its tip. It can be extended up toward the level of the back, indicating excitement, but is not used for communication purposes to the same extent as in the case of some other breeds such as Terriers. Instead, the tail is generally used as a counterbalance when running.

GREYHOUND RACING

First attempts to race Greyhounds took place during 1876 in London, England, on a straight track, but racing did not become popular until the 1920s. Racing Greyhounds chase a mechanical hare around what has now become a curved track. Show Greyhounds, in contrast, are bred to be exhibited, rather than raced.

Racing ahead This Greyhound's deep chest provides a good lung capacity, helping to meet its oxygen requirement when running at full speed, while its long legs enable it to cover ground quickly.

SAFETY FIRST

Retired Greyhounds make excellent pets, being quiet and gentle by nature. They should be muzzled when out walking, though, as they may chase and injure small dogs and cats.

Scenthounds

Scenthounds are a much more recent development than sighthounds (see pages 152–153). They were created for a different type of hunting, popular as an aristocratic pursuit during medieval times, from about 1,000 years ago. The first scenthound was the St. Hubert Hound, ancestor of today's Bloodhound.

French origins

Hunting with hounds became a popular pastime in medieval France, with individual packs evolving around the different chateaux. There could be several forms of the same basic breed, differing in terms of size and coat type. A significant mutation that arose in this area of Europe resulted in the emergence of what are now known as Basset breeds. The name derives from the French word *bas*, meaning "low," referring to the short stature of these hounds.

Their short legs mean that Bassets are typically accompanied on foot, rather than by riders, and usually hunt smaller quarry such as rabbits and hares, rather than the wild boar that their larger counterparts pursued. The social chaos of the French Revolution (1789–1799) saw many of the localized breeds of scenthounds wiped out, along with their aristocratic owners. However, a small number survived, and today the Basset breeds have become popular as pets.

Unchanging role Foxhounds have always been kept exclusively for the purpose for which they were originally bred. They have never entered the show ring, nor are they kept as pets, even today.

FOXHOUNDS

The tradition of foxhunting began in England, and pedigree records of different packs extend back much farther than in the case of show dogs. Foxhounds were taken overseas as well, and in the U.S. they were used to create not just the American Foxhound, but they also contributed to the ancestry of some Coonhound breeds (see page 137).

White tip The Bassett Hound's tail typically has a white tip so the dog can be seen by the hunters.

Exuberant companions
The typical behavior of scenthounds is a direct result of their lifestyle, as they need plenty of exercise. Although social by nature, they tend to form a pack hierarchy when living together. This reflects their Gray Wolf ancestry, although in terms of temperament they are completely different. Gone is the innate shyness of the wolf, replaced by a natural exuberance, and this makes these hounds appealing as pets. They are very friendly and generally accepting of people, so they do not generally make good guardians.

Overenthusiasm
Scenthounds love to be part of a group, and this makes them an ideal choice for a home with teenage children who have corresponding amounts of energy when it comes to playing games. Scenthounds often use their tails to indicate excitement, wagging them enthusiastically. Training a scenthound is not as straightforward as for many breeds, however, because of the way that they hunt. They will detect a scent, head off on the trail of it, and be almost impossible to recall.

Unique skill Bloodhounds are prized for their ability to track "cold scents"—trails left by their quarry days ago. In spite of their fitness, though, studies have shown that this breed is one of the most short-lived.

Trapping smells The Bloodhound's long, pendulous ears trap scent molecules close to the nose, as do the skin folds around the neck.

SAFETY FIRST
Never feed any dog before exercise. This can lead to bloat, which is often fatal (see page 10).

Coat types
Not all Bassets—or indeed scenthounds of larger stature—have smooth, short coats. There are a number of rough-coated Bassets, for example, the Basset Fauve de Bretagne, which is descended from the longer-legged Griffon Fauve de Bretagne.

The wiry nature of the coats of such scenthounds helps protect them from injury when running through undergrowth in pursuit of quarry. The coat also does not become matted—an advantage because these dogs were bred to hunt in packs, rather than as pets. It makes it much easier for them to be cared for as part of a group.

Search and rescue

Dogs have been used for centuries to find people who have become lost—often as the result of adverse weather conditions—due to their ability to locate the source of scent molecules present in the air. They also help locate earthquake victims and people trapped in train crashes.

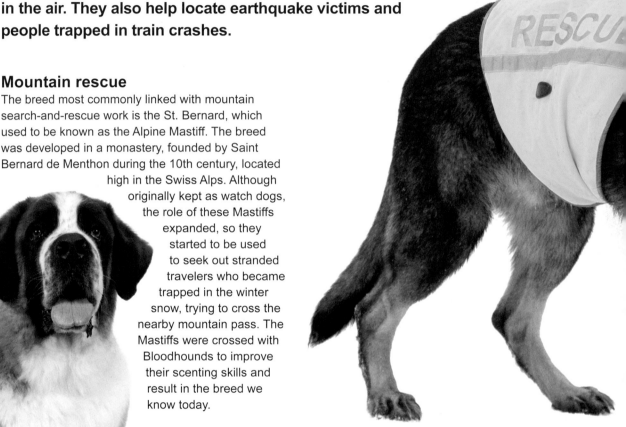

Mountain rescue

The breed most commonly linked with mountain search-and-rescue work is the St. Bernard, which used to be known as the Alpine Mastiff. The breed was developed in a monastery, founded by Saint Bernard de Menthon during the 10th century, located high in the Swiss Alps. Although originally kept as watch dogs, the role of these Mastiffs expanded, so they started to be used to seek out stranded travelers who became trapped in the winter snow, trying to cross the nearby mountain pass. The Mastiffs were crossed with Bloodhounds to improve their scenting skills and result in the breed we know today.

Myth St. Bernards never actually carried miniature kegs of brandy to revive frozen travelers. This belief arose as the result of a painting showing this by Queen Victoria's favorite animal painter, Sir Edwin Landseer (1802–1873). It was entitled *Alpine Mastiff Reanimating a Distressed Traveler*.

Livesavers

St. Bernards continued to perform their mountain-rescue task for centuries, with the most famous individual of all being Barry, who saved some 40 people from certain death between 1800 and 1812. A legacy still exists from that early era, when St. Bernards were crossed with Newfoundlands. Even today, some of these dogs display thicker, longer coats than others. It was thought that they would be better suited to tracking in the bitterly cold Alpine conditions. Although the breed is no longer kept for this purpose today, these dogs are credited with rescuing about 2,000 lost travelers in total.

Avalanche rescue
In Switzerland, German Shepherds have been used since the late 1930s to locate avalanche victims. Training centers are now common throughout the Alpine region.

Volunteer teams

In potentially hazardous areas of countryside that are popular with hikers and climbers, there are mountain rescue teams run by volunteers who have specially trained dogs. They will go out in bad weather to find any lost or missing people and also to help the emergency services in the event of any accident. A variety of dogs are used in such cases, and not always purebreds, although Labrador Retrievers and Border Collies are most frequently used.

Tough training

The training for rescue dogs is very difficult, and it typically takes two or three years for a dog to reach the required standard. It starts by learning to pick up the scent of a person in the air, barking loudly and running backward and forward to their handler, and helping guide the search team directly to the missing person, who may be unconscious and unable to call out. For training purposes, though, the person being "found" praises the dog, to give it encouragement.

Out to work

Both the dog and its handler have to pass a number of formal assessments to be accepted, and regular ongoing assessments are made as long as they remain part of the team. Such training has also proved successful following natural disasters that have resulted in the collapse of buildings, resulting in people being trapped. Search-and-rescue dogs are flown out to such localities to help find survivors in these areas. They work in a similar way as they would in the open, being able to detect human breath, skin cells, and perspiration.

CRIME-SCENE SKILLS

Since search and rescue dogs sometimes locate bodies, part of the training program involves learning not to destroy potential evidence at crime scenes. In some cases, dogs and their handlers are called in by the police to assist in searching for missing persons in open countryside. These dogs must be able to pick up the scent of a person even under the snow.

Sled dogs

Sled dogs bear the closest resemblance, of all of domestic dogs, to their wolf ancestors. They provide a transportation lifeline for communities throughout the Arctic region. Even today, they can often prove more dependable than mechanical means of transportation.

Pack organization

Working outdoors in groups, in what are frequently bitterly cold surroundings and harsh terrain, Sled dogs typically retain strong pack instincts. There is an evident hierarchy within a group, mirroring that of a wolf pack. This is reflected in the way the musher (sled driver) uses the dogs. They are not harnessed randomly—the lead dog at the front is the dominant member of the team and probably also the most experienced. The dogs are not just organized in this way for canine compatibility, but also for the safety of all concerned. The other dogs will follow the pack leader, and his expertise should help them all avoid potential dangers.

Striking eyes This Husky puppy has blue eyes—a feature often associated with the breed.

Multitasking Sled dogs can be surprisingly versatile. The Samoyed, seen here, doubles up as a reindeer herder, confirming the intelligence and adaptability of these dogs.

SAFETY FIRST

Sled dogs are naturally powerful and will instinctively pull. Aim to control this behavior when training your puppy.

RACING SLED DOGS

There are races organized for owners of working Sled dogs. In some northern countries where snow is not present all year round, teams compete by pulling carts instead of sleds.

Adapted to the cold The Samoyed's outer coat is very weather-resistant, and it also has a dense undercoat, which helps trap the warmth from the dog's body close to the skin. The long, curled tail is tucked over the dog's face when it sleeps curled up, helping to keep its head warm.

Recreational Sled dog The Chinook is quite a scarce breed and tends to be kept mainly as a pet, although it may be used for recreational sledding.

Toe warmers Many Sled dogs have fur that helps protect the pads of their feet from frozen ground underfoot.

A new addition

Not all Sled dogs were developed in the far north or are of ancient lineage. The Chinook (above), recognized as New Hampshire's state dog, has existed for less than a century. It was conceived and created by Arthur Walden, a resident of that state who was also a very experienced dog sledder. He had a favorite lead dog named Chinook, bred from a cross between a Husky and a Mastiff-type dog, and decided to try to create a breed based on this dog's appearance.

Chinook himself had a sad end, dying on an expedition to the Antarctic during the 1920s when Sled dogs were used for exploration purposes there, but the breed has continued to the present day. Such dogs have a reputation for being calm and friendly, with the Mastiff influence being clearly apparent in their ear shape and saberlike tail, which are quite different from those of other sled breeds.

Water dogs

A number of different breeds have adapted to work in and around water. All dogs can swim well, and this characteristic has also been exploited in recent times by the development of hydrotherapy for dogs suffering from muscular and skeletal problems.

Swimming technique

Dogs have been created to work in rivers and lakes and also out at sea. Many of these breeds share a common ancestry. Some also display specific adaptations for working in this type of environment, including webbing between the toes. This enables them to swim more efficiently, like the feet of waterfowl.

Water retrievers

Dogs have been employed since the Middle Ages to retrieve shot waterfowl from lakes, rivers, and marshes (see pages 150–151). The lineage of these dogs today is typically represented by the Poodle, as well as the Irish Water Spaniel, both of which are descended from the Barbet, a breed that is now rare. Breeds descended from the Barbet can be recognized by their curly coats. Another example is the Curly-coated Retriever, with the extinct English Water Spaniel, the Irish Water Spaniel, and the Poodle all having contributed to its ancestry.

Thick tails Dogs that work in water have broad, thick tails to help them swim in the right direction.

Clever coat The Labradoodle's curly coat is water repellent, while at the same time trapping warm air close to the body. These dogs were developed as hypoallergenic guide dogs, because they do not shed much hair.

Designer appearance

It is obviously important that a dog retrieving game can swim easily and yet will not succumb to the cold water. The coat styling of exhibition Poodles is very precise and may look fancy, but this type of trim can be traced back to their working ancestry. The untrimmed areas on the body help keep in warmth, and the joints are protected by fur. Shaving parts of the legs lessens the water resistance when the dog is swimming, which therefore demands less energy. The fur at the tip of the tail is left in a pompom, so the dog can be spotted easily in the water. Pet poodles are now usually left in what is described as a "lamb clip," with even fur over their entire bodies.

True companions

It is no coincidence that many water Retrievers have become popular as pets, because these dogs have evolved to work closely alongside people. The most popular of the crosses between different purebred dogs is now the Labradoodle, the result of combining Labrador Retriever and Poodle bloodlines, with its intelligent, obedient nature and friendly disposition. The results were originally quite variable, tending to favor one parent, but Labradoodle pairings now result in puppies with a more standard appearance.

Life jacket
Even dogs that are excellent swimmers should wear a life jacket if you take them out in a boat.

SWIMMING TECHNIQUE

All dogs, whether used to the water or not, employ a similar technique when swimming, often described as "dog paddling," even when replicated by human swimmers. They swim along, apparently using their front feet, though it is actually the power of their well-muscled hindquarters that provides them with forward propulsion. The dog will be quite low in the water, but its nose is kept above the surface. Its tail acts like a rudder, helping it steer.

Drying off

Labradoodles and their ancestors have a particular affinity for water and will delight in having the opportunity to swim, but give your pet plenty of space when it emerges back onto dry land. It will shake itself dry, in a very distinctive manner, effectively rolling its body from side to side at speed, and causing water to spray out of its water-resistant coat over a surprisingly wide area. Having shaken itself in this way to remove most of the water, the remainder will evaporate quite quickly from the coat. This quick drying helps guard against the dog becoming chilled in cold weather. Even so, you may want to dry your dog with a towel after it has shaken itself, especially if you are taking it home in a car. If a dog has been in the ocean, bathing it when you get back home to remove excess salt deposits from the coat is recommended (see page 108).

Military dogs

Dogs have a long history in military service, extending back over many centuries. They have undertaken a variety of tasks, from pulling ammunition carts to acting as messengers, but their roles have changed with the nature of warfare. More recent tasks include the detection of hidden improvised explosive devices.

On the battlefield

In the past, dogs were used in actual combat, but with the advent of gunpowder, their direct involvement on the battlefield came to end. Contemporary accounts suggested they could be a liability in the chaos of the fighting in any event, sometimes even turning on soldiers on their own side. Fierce Mastiff-type dogs were used, which were reputedly bigger and were definitely more aggressive than similar breeds today.

Historical legacy

There is a direct link right back to this era, though, extending to the Battle of Agincourt, which took place in 1415 between the British and French armies. Sir Peers Legh, Knight of Lyme Hall, in the English county of Cheshire, was mortally wounded but was guarded loyally by his favorite Mastiff. After the battle, the dog was taken back to Cheshire and founded the Lyme Hall bloodline, which is still represented in pedigree Mastiffs today.

Military stalwart
The German Shepherd has proved to be one of the most popular breeds used by the armed services.

ARMY TRAINING

Dogs are carefully trained for their diverse roles in the military, working very closely alongside their handlers. Not all dogs make the grade, however—just as among human military recruits. A surprisingly high number of those used by the military are actually unwanted pets from animal rescue centers.

World War I

During World War I, some dogs were trained as guardians on the lookout for saboteurs, while others acted as messengers. They were especially well suited to being messengers, because they could run quickly through the mud and in the trenches, at a time when battlefield communications were relatively primitive. They also helped provide a boost to morale among the troops, particularly those on the front line.

Subsequent service

In subsequent conflicts, dogs played an even more diverse range of roles. They have been parachuted out of planes to work with their handlers, alerted troops to the presence of minefields, and searched for weapons, as well as guarding key military installations. Out on patrol, they have been able to alert soldiers to the whereabouts of the enemy.

This was one of their key tasks during the Vietnam War, where more than 4,000 military working dogs, as they were officially known, saw active service. In the past, service regulations stated that these dogs had to be euthanized when their working lives ended, but these days they are rehomed.

SAFETY FIRST

Veterinary care is very important for dogs working in areas where they may be exposed to new diseases and parasites.

Dogs in the armed forces today

The abilities of dogs are still highly valued by the armed services today and have saved countless lives in recent conflicts in Iraq and Afghanistan.

One such incident involved Buster, a five-year-old Springer Spaniel. Shortly after the fall of Baghdad, British troops were trying to quell an insurgency in the southern town of Safwan. A careful search had failed to uncover any munitions, but Buster's scenting skills soon revealed a large cache of arms and ammunition, as well as drugs, that were hidden in a wall cavity. Arrests followed and, as a direct result of Buster's success, the area became peaceful once again. For his bravery throughout the campaign, he was awarded the Dickin Medal, honoring the work of animals in war.

Ever alert Ear cropping can make breeds, such as the Doberman seen here, appear more aggressive and intimidating when used in military service, although this surgery is now outlawed in many countries.

Drug detection

The scenting abilities of dogs have been used in different situations, and it has proved possible to use trained dogs in the front-line battle against illegal drug trafficking. In fact, so successful have particular dogs been that drug gangs are reputed to have placed a bounty on them.

Getting the scent Dogs are encouraged to run over passenger bags laid flat as their weight forces out the scent of hidden drugs.

Key attributes

The selection process begins with dogs that are between one and three years old and still have a good working life in front of them, as training these dogs is expensive. They are thoroughly screened for any potential health problems that could compromise their working ability and are then tested for their suitability. Working under pressure, drug detection dogs require good powers of concentration, so they will not be easily distracted by what is going on around them—in a cargo shed, for example, or when sniffing bags on an airport carousel.

A partnership

There is a very strong link between the dog and its handler from the outset. Dogs are not usually switched between handlers, instead working as a close team to achieve the best results.

The breeds to use

Different breeds have been trained for detecting drugs, with Spaniels and Retrievers having worked very successfully in this role. They are often preferred over more traditional scenthounds, simply because they are instinctively better suited to working on a one-to-one basis with people. Purebred dogs tend to be favored, simply because they often have better specialist scent-detection skills than nonpedigrees, but crossbreeds have been used for this work as well.

SAFETY FIRST

Dogs can be badly affected if they consume cannabis. They are initially excitable, then lose coordination, before becoming drowsy.

Initial training

One of the most common tests used to determine whether a dog has the aptitude to become an efficient drug detector is to watch its reaction when a ball is bounced in front of it. Dogs that focus on the ball, rather than the person, are chosen because this demonstrates good powers of concentration. Their initial training is often based on recognizing cannabis. It can take six weeks on average for a dog to master this skill, being first of all trained with a small amount of the drug hidden in a towel.

Progression

Once the dog has shown its potential and passed a rigorous test, it is then likely to learn how to recognize other drugs, such as heroin. Not all dogs manage to reach the top level of training. Those that fail will leave the program and be rehomed. Each handler starts off working with two dogs, simply because a significant number will not complete their training successfully.

Concealed response

It is important for only the handler to understand that a dog has detected drugs in a consignment, so as not to alert any smugglers who may be watching. When it comes to catching criminals, so-called "passive dogs"—which will sit and subtly indicate the presence of drugs, rather than rushing up to the person concerned—are used.

HIGHLY VERSATILE

One of the reasons dogs are used for detecting drugs is that they can be employed in a wide range of locations, and this itself can act as a deterrent. They can be used not just at airports, but also at docks, checking incoming containers of freight, which are a favored route for the smuggling of bulk consignments of drugs.

Flawed candidate
Bloodhounds are not used to detect drugs, despite their obvious capabilities. The problem is that they will want to follow a scent, rather than simply revealing that they have detected it.

Cancer detectors

The scenting skills of dogs have been recognized for centuries, but only recently has their ability to detect cancers in people become apparent. This remarkable skill has now become the subject of serious interest from medical scientists and has helped shed new light on various cancers.

Early indicator of ability

Studies in this area began during the late 1980s following the case of a Dalmatian named Trude, who persistently attempted to nibble a mole off the leg of her owner. He went to his doctor and was shocked to discover that the skin blemish was, in fact, a malignant melanoma—a highly dangerous cancer. The case attracted headlines around the world, and other instances of dogs alerting their owners to similar conditions soon came to light.

Breast cancer diagnosis

One of the most interesting cases involved a dog that warned its owner that she had breast cancer by persistently trying to reach the affected area. Once the tumor was removed, the dog's behavior returned to normal for a time, but it started to behave in a similar way again about three months later. A subsequent check-up revealed that a small area of cancerous tissue was still present in the woman's breast. Research findings in the U.S. and the U.K. soon revealed that dogs could be trained to detect various cancers. It has also emerged that changes in the breath of a person suffering from breast cancer may alert the dog to the problem.

Too much information?

With their highly developed sense of smell, you might think that dogs could be faced with detecting so many scents as to cause confusion but, in fact, they perceive smells differently than we do. We smell a curry, for example, as a distinctive odor, but dogs actually detect the different scents of the individual spices, and possess the ability to distinguish one curry from another on this basis. Their brain is highly developed in terms of processing and interpreting olfactory information (see page 104).

Simple technique
Clicker training, as is often used for obedience work, has been adopted to train dogs working in this field. The dog is given a click from the clicker device when it responds correctly, to let it know what is required of it.

Training for the task

In some cases, dogs have clearly been able to pick up an abnormality in their owner without any training. Scientists have since worked with experienced dog handlers to see if there are ways to train dogs to detect the presence of cancerous cells from samples. The results have been remarkable, as typified by the case of George, a Standard Schnauzer, who took part in a trial in Tallahassee, Florida. Having previously been trained to detect explosives, George had no difficulty in detecting skin cancer by scent, achieving a success rate of 99 percent.

Detecting different cancers

In the U.K., dogs have been trained to detect bladder cancer from urine samples and, although the success rate was not as high as in George's case, it was significantly higher than it would have been otherwise. More importantly, the dogs had a higher success rate during the early stages of this disease than established means of diagnosis, such as computerized axial tomography (CAT) scanning. Breath samples have also been used, with dogs once again showing that they possess the ability to detect not just breast cancer, but also lung cancer.

It has also emerged that some dogs are more talented in this diagnostic field than others.

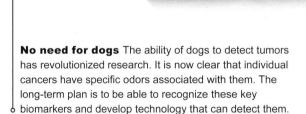

No need for dogs The ability of dogs to detect tumors has revolutionized research. It is now clear that individual cancers have specific odors associated with them. The long-term plan is to be able to recognize these key biomarkers and develop technology that can detect them.

CANCER-DETECTING CLONES

Being spayed meant that Marine, a Labrador Retriever in Japan—who displayed exceptional talent when it came to detecting cancer—could not have puppies. As a result, she has now been cloned in South Korea, and scientists hope that, as with drug-sniffing dogs cloned previously, Marine's puppies will have inherited her skill.

SAFETY FIRST

Bitches can themselves be vulnerable to breast cancer. If you detect any lumps on your pet, seek veterinary advice without delay.

The learning process The training of successful cancer-detecting dogs follows a very similar method to that used for teaching dogs to recognize the scent of drugs or explosives. Dogs can recognize specific scents, enabling them to focus on detecting bladder rather than prostate cancer in a urine sample, for example.

Glossary

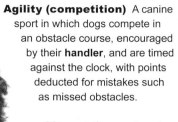

Agility (competition) A canine sport in which dogs compete in an obstacle course, encouraged by their **handler**, and are timed against the clock, with points deducted for mistakes such as missed obstacles.

Altered See **neutered**.

Antibodies Protective proteins present in the blood and bodily fluids that form a critical part of the immune system, protecting against infections. The development of antibodies can be triggered by **vaccination** or as the result of an actual **infection**.

Barking The characteristic vocalization of a dog, which serves as a warning, often being intimidatory. Barking is a feature of most domestic dogs, with some breeds barking more frequently than others.

Baying The very distinctive, melodic calls uttered by a scenthound when it is following a trail. This far-carrying call keeps members of the pack in touch with each other.

Bitch The term used to describe a female dog.

Bloat The result of an unnatural accumulation of gas in the stomach, causing it to become swollen, with the possible consequence of causing the stomach to twist ("gastric torsion"). It is a particular problem in large, deep-chested breeds, such as Great Danes. Feeding prior to exercise can be a contributing factor to this potentially life-threatening condition.

Bloodline The ancestry of a particular dog, extending back over numerous generations.

Bobtail A naturally occurring greatly reduced tail length, typically associated with herding breeds, such as Old English Sheepdogs.

Body language A means of communication that relies on body posturing, often used in conjunction with other, direct indicators of a dog's mood, such as **growling** or other forms of **vocalization**.

Breed A clearly recognizable type of dog, characterized and distinguished by its appearance, as defined by its breed standard (the characteristics that define a breed, set by the kennel club).

Caching The way in which wild dogs hide food, particularly when they have too much, with the aim of protecting it from predators so they can return to eat it later.

Canids A general description used for all members of the family Canidae, including wolves, coyotes, foxes, jackals, and the domestic dog.

Designer dog The labradoodle—a cross between a labrador and poodle, was one of the original "designer dogs."

Canine As well as a broad term for dogs, it is an adjective typically describing canine behavior. It is also the name given to the long, pointed tooth present at each corner of the mouth, behind the incisors.

Canine behaviorist A person who studies the behavior of **canids**, typically domestic dogs, and helps overcome behavioral difficulties.

Carnassial teeth Represented by a combination of the last premolar tooth in the upper jaw and the first molar in the lower jaw. Working together, these teeth have a shearing action, helping dismantle prey.

Crossbreeding Mating between two different breeds. This has become more widespread, serving as the basis for creating **designer dogs**. Puppies produced by crossbreeding are likely to be variable in appearance.

Designer dogs A current trend which has the aim of creating dogs with specific characteristics, such as hypoallergenic dogs, by **crossbreeding**. The best-known designer dog is the Labradoodle, bred originally from pairings between Labrador Retrievers and Poodles.

Dingo A primitive form of **feral** dog found in Australia, which is persecuted because it is regarded as a menace by sheep farmers. It has hybridized increasingly with its domestic relatives in recent years.

Distemper A potentially fatal viral illness in dogs, easily preventable by **vaccination**. Dogs that do recover from distemper can suffer complications later in life.

DNA An abbreviation for deoxyribonucleic acid. DNA is the genetic basis or blueprint for the appearance of virtually all life-forms (apart from some viruses), encoding all the characteristics of the organism in its double-helix structure.

Docking The removal of a variable amount of a puppy's tail soon after birth. Originally to protect working dogs from injuries, it has now been outlawed in many countries.

Domestication
The process whereby a wild animal becomes used to living in harmony with people, through breeding.

Dominant An assertive individual or a genetic trait that can become evident in the first generation of puppies.

Ear cropping Cutting of the ear of puppies so the remaining cartilage causes them to stick up. Breeds treated in this way include the Doberman and Great Dane, but this practice is outlawed in many countries.

Epilepsy A convulsive disorder that results in unpredictable seizures.

Feral Dogs that are not domesticated or that have reverted to a free-living existence, scavenging around human settlements rather than hunting.

Gastric torsion See **Bloat**.

Genetic A characteristic encoded in the genes that is passed from one generation to the next.

Gestation period The length of time that pregnancy lasts—typically 63 days in dogs.

Gland An organ in the body that produces a chemical that will act elsewhere in the body, typically being carried in the bloodstream (endocrine glands); releases a secretion onto the skin (e.g., sweat glands); or produces milk (mammary glands).

Grooming The process of maintaining a dog's coat, which may include techniques such as stripping as well as brushing and combing.

Growling A low rumbling sound uttered by a dog as a warning that increases in frequency if ignored.

Guardian A dog that protects people or property, such as a sheepdog.

Gun dog A dog used to retrieve game.

Hackles The area of fur along the back at the base of the neck, which can be raised by the dog as a warning gesture, accompanied by **growling** or **barking**.

Handler The person responsible for accompanying the dog on a walk or when it is taking part in other activities, such as an **agility** competition.

Heat The period during the bitch's reproductive cycle when she is ovulating, or releasing eggs from her ovaries (also known as estrus). Most domestic dogs have two periods of heat annually.

Heel work A dog is trained to walk at the heels of its **handler**.

Herding dogs Dogs whose primary function is to herd livestock, typically sheep and cattle.

Hindquarters The rear part of the dog, including the muscular hind legs.

Howling A far-carrying call often uttered by wolves, typically audible over a long distance, and most commonly used by **sled dogs**.

House broken A dog that has been trained not to soil in the home.

Hybrid The progeny of a mating between two distinctive species.

Incursion Movement into another dog's territory.

Infection An attack on the body's immune system, by a bacterium, virus, or parasite, which can create symptoms of a disease.

Lamb clip A basic trim of a Poodle's coat, looking similar in appearance to the coat of a lamb.

Lap dogs Small dogs that are kept exclusively in the home as companions and are so-called because they are small enough to sit on their owner's lap.

Litter A group of puppies born to a bitch at one time.

Microchipped The use of a microchip containing a unique code, inserted under the skin of the dog's neck, which will serve to identify it if it gets lost or strays. The chip is activated by a special reader.

Muscle tone The strength and bulk of the muscle. Muscle tone decreases in the case of less active dogs.

Muzzle The front part of the dog's face, including the nose, being significantly longer in some breeds, such as the Greyhound, compared with others, like the Pug.

Neutered A dog that has undergone surgery to prevent it from being able to breed. This is known as castration in male dogs, and as spaying in bitches.

Obedience training The way in which a dog is trained to follow the commands of its **handler**.

Pack A group of dogs or other **canids**.

Pads The area that is free of hair on the underside of the dog's paws.

Parasites Organisms found on or in the dog's body that cause it harm, while benefiting themselves.

Patellar luxation A weakness of the knee-cap or patella, typically seen in small breeds of dogs, causing it to dislocate readily. This is usually a congenital problem (existing from birth) and is likely to require surgical correction.

Pheromones Chemical messengers that are produced in small amounts and wafted on air currents. Used by a bitch to attract male dogs when she is in **heat**.

Play fighting The way in which two dogs that know each other well will engage in mock fights together, without causing injuries. Such behavior is most likely to be seen in puppies.

Pointers A breed of **gun dog**.

Predatory Hunting instincts displayed by a species (a predator) in search of prey.

Regurgitated Brought back up the esophagus (the gullet)—bitches will regurgitate solid food when weaning their puppies.

Rehoming Finding a new, permanent home for puppies or older dogs.

REM sleep The "rapid eye movement" phase of sleep, when a dog may be seen twitching, although it is sleeping soundly.

Retrievers A group of breeds used originally as gun dogs to retrieve shot waterfowl but now employed for a much wider range of tasks.

Salivation The increased output of saliva by the salivary **glands** in the mouth.

Scavenger Obtaining food that has been discarded or left rather than actively hunting for prey.

Scenthounds A group of hounds, including the Beagle, that track their quarry primarily by scent.

Scentmarking The use of urine, sweat, feces, and anal gland secretions to mark an area.

Secretion The output of a chemical from a **gland** or cell which has a useful function.

Sighthounds Hounds, such as the Greyhound, that use their sharp eyesight to detect prey and then rely on their speed to catch the creature.

Sled dogs Breeds such as the Siberian Husky that have been used for centuries in the Arctic to pull sleds, providing a vital means of communication in such areas.

Snarling The way in which dogs curl their lips as a warning, exposing their teeth and **growling** at the same time.

Social hierarchy The organization or structure of dogs within a pack, with some individuals being **dominant**.

Socialization The need for young puppies to experience and explore their environment from an early age, to prevent them from being nervous later.

Stamina A dog's physical strength and endurance.

Stray A dog which has no owner and is living on the streets, scavenging for food.

Teats The swollen areas on the underside of the bitch's body, where puppies suckle in order to obtain milk. Most dogs have ten teats, but small breeds may not have as many.

Territorial A protective attitude toward a territory, such as a dog defending the home from an intruder.

Ultrasound Sound that is above the typical upper frequency level of 20,000 hertz audible to humans, but which nevertheless can still be heard by dogs.

Weaning Puppies are generally weaned onto solid food from between the fourth and sixth week.

Underparts The lower side of the dog's body, running from the chin along the chest to the abdomen.

Vaccination The use of a vaccine to stimulate the body's immune response and protect against an infection. Annual boosters are necessary to maintain an effective level of protective cover.

Vascular Tissue with a very good blood supply.

Vocalization Any noise emanating from the dog's vocal chords.

Weaning The process whereby a puppy switches from its mother's milk to relying entirely on solid food for nutritional purposes.

Whelping To give birth to puppies.

Whining A repetitive call made by domestic dogs when they are having difficulty attracting attention.

Withers The highest point of the shoulder, and the level that serves as the standard benchmark when measuring the height of dogs.

Working breed A large breed of dog created to work alongside people, such as a guard dog like a Rottweiler or a **sled dog** like a Samoyed.

Further Reading and Resources

Further Reading

Alderton, David. *How to Talk with Your Dog*. Howell Book House, 2000.

Alderton, David. *Your Dog Interpreter*. Reader's Digest, 2007.

Alderton, David. *Smithsonian Handbooks: Dogs*. Covent Garden Books, 2009.

American Kennel Club, The. *The Complete Dog Book*. Ballantine Books, 2006.

Baer, Ted. *Communicating with Your Dog: A Humane Approach to Dog Training*. Barron's Educational Series, 1999.

Canadian Kennel Club, The. *The Canadian Kennel Club Book of Dogs*. Stoddard Publishing, 1988.

Combe, De Prisco, Andrew & Johnson, James B. *Canine Lexicon*. TFH Publications, 1993.

Gagne, Tammy. *Designer Dogs: Animal Planet™ Pet Care Library*. TFH Publications, 2008.

Jackson, Frank. *The Dictionary of Canine Terms*. Crowood Press, 1995.

Kennel Club, The. *The Kennel Club's Illustrated Breed Standards*. Ebury Press, 1998.

Leach, Laurie. *The Beginner's Guide to Dog Agility*. TFH Publications, 2006.

Leach, Laurie. *The Intermediate's Guide to Dog Agility: Take Your Game to the Next Level*. TFH Publications, 2010.

Lindsay, Steven R. *Handbook of Applied Dog Behavior and Training, Volume 1: Adaptation and Learning*. Iowa State University Press, 2000.

Lindsay, Steven R. *Handbook of Applied Dog Behavior and Training, Volume 2: Etiology and Assessment of Behavior Problems*. Iowa State University Press, 2001.

Miklósi, Adam. *Dog Behavior, Evolution and Cognition*. Oxford University Press, U.S.A., 2009.

Serpell, James. *The Domestic Dog: Its Evolution, Behaviour, and Interactions With People*. Cambridge University Press, 1996.

Sanderson, Angela. *The Complete Book of Australian Dogs*. The Currawong Press, 1981.

Wilcox, Bonnie & Walkowicz, Chris. *The Atlas of Dog Breeds of the World*. TFH Publications, 1989.

Yarden, C. Miriam. *Hey Pup, Let's Talk!* Barron's Educational Series, 2000.

Major breed registries in North America and Canada

American Kennel Club, 260 Madison Avenue, New York, NY 10016, U.S.A.
www.akc.org

Canadian Kennel Club, 89 Skyway Avenue, Suite 100, Etobicoke, Ontario M9W 6R4, Canada.
www.ckc.ca

Continental Kennel Club, PO Box 1628, Walker, LA 70785, U.S.A.
www.continentalkennelclub.com

National Kennel Club, 255 Indian Ridge Road, PO 331, Blaine, Tennessee 37709, U.S.A.
www.nationalkennelclub.com

United Kennel Club, 100 East Kilgore Road, Kalamazoo, MI 49002, U.S.A.
www.ukcdogs.com

Universal Kennel Club International, PO 574, Nanuet, NY 10954, U.S.A.
www.universalkennel.com

World Kennel Club, PO Box 60771, Oklahoma City, OK 73146, U.S.A. www.worldkennelclub.com

World Wide Kennel Club, PO Box 62, Mount Vernon, NY 10552, U.S.A. www.worldwidekennel.qpg.com

Major breed registries in Europe, Africa, Asia, and Australia

Australian National Kennel Council, PO Box 285, Red Hill South, Victoria 3937, Australia. www.ankc.org.au

Fédération Cynologique Int., Place Albert 1er, 13 B-6530 Thuin, Belgium. www.fci.be

Irish Kennel Club, Fottrell House, Harold's Cross Bridge, Dublin 6W, Republic of Ireland. www.ikc.ie

The Kennel Club, 1–5 Clarges Street, London, W1Y 8AB, England. www.thekennelclub.org.uk

The Kennel Club of India, Old No.89, New No.28, AA-Block, 1st Street, Anna Nagar, Chennai-600040, India. www.dogsindia.com/registered_kennel_clubs_in_india.htm

The Kennel Union of South Africa (formerly The South African Kennel Club), P.O. Box 2659, Cape Town 8000, South Africa. www.kusa.co.za

New Zealand Kennel Club, Prosser Street, Private Bag 50903, Porirua 6220, New Zealand. www.nzkc.org.nz

Index

Acknowledgments

Marshall Editions would like to thank the following agencies for supplying images for inclusion in this book:

Key: **t** = top **b** = bottom **c** = center **r** = right **l** = left

Front cover: Shutterstock/Foto Jagodka
Back cover: Shutterstock/Roman Sigaev

Pages: 1 iStock/GlobalP; **2–3** Warren Photographic/Mark Taylor; **4–5** Shutterstock/Erik Lam; **6** iStock/GlobalP; **7t** Warren Photographic/Jane Burton; **7c** Warren Photographic/Jane Burton; **7b** iStock /Stephanie Phillips; **8–9** Corbis/ Jim Craigmyle; **10** Warren Photographic/Mark Taylor; **11** Animal Photography/David Jensen; **12** Shutterstock/Timophey_V_P; **13** DK Images/Dave King; **14** Warren Photographic/Jane Burton; **15b** Shutterstock/Viorel Sima; **15t** DK Images/Jerry Young; **16b** Getty/ Anderson Ross; **16t** Animal Photography/Sally Anne Thompson; **17t** Shutterstock/ifong; **17b** Shutterstock/Gelpi; **18t** Shutterstock/Willee Cole; **18b** Shutterstock/Lukas Zfus; **19** Shutterstock/Studio Foxy; **20t** Shutterstock/Liliya Kulianionak; **20c** Shutterstock/Erik Lam; **21** Shutterstock/Dorling Kindersley; **22** Animal Photography/Tetsu Yamazaki; **23** Shutterstock/Lobke Peers; **24t** DK Images/Tracy Morgan; **24c** DK Images/Dorling Kindersley; **25t** Getty/Martin Harvey; **26b** Warren Photographic/Jane Burton; **26c** Shutterstock/Jean Frooms; **27t** Warren Photographic/Mark Taylor; **28** Warren Photographic/Jane Burton; **29t** Animal Photography/Barbara O'Brien; **29b** Shutterstock/Margo Harrison; **30t** Warren Photographic/Jane Burton; **30c** Shutterstock/Utekhina Anna; **31b** Animal Photography/Anita Peeples; **32** Warren Photographic/ Jane Burton; **33t** Warren Photographic/Jane Burton; **33b** Shutterstock/Willee Cole; **34b** Shutterstock/Zodrev Kirill Vladimirovich; **34c** Shutterstock/J. Paget, R. F. Photos; **35b** Shutterstock/Viorel Sima; **36b** Warren Photographic/Jane Burton; **36c** Warren Photographic/Mark Taylor; **37** DK Images/Emma Firth; **38** Getty/G.K. Hart/Vikki Hart; **39** Warren Photographic/Jane Burton; **40–41** Shutterstock/Vitaly Titov and Maria Sidelnikova; **42** Animal Photography/Barbara O'Brien; **43t** Corbis/Joe McDonald **43b** Animal Photography/Martin Harvey; **44b** Shutterstock/Eric Isselée; **44c** Shutterstock/Maxim Kulko; **45t** Shutterstock/Torsten Lorenz; **45b** Shutterstock/Eric Isselée; **46t** Shutterstock/Chris Alcock; **46c** Warren Photographic/Jane Burton; **47t** Shutterstock/Maxim Kulko; **47b** Warren Photographic/Jane Burton; **48t** Warren Photographic/Mark Taylor; **48b** Shutterstock/Eric Isselée; **49t** Shutterstock/Eric Isselée; **49b** Shutterstock/Alexia Khruscheva; **50t** Shutterstock/Eric Isselée; **50b** Warren Photographic/Jane Burton; **51t** Shutterstock/Erik Lam; **51c** Shutterstock/Eric Isselée; **51b** Shutterstock/Dr. Margorius; **52t** Shutterstock/Foto Jagodka; **52b** Shutterstock/Annette Shaff; **53t** Shutterstock/Annette Shaff; **53bl** Shutterstock/Eric Isselée; **53br** Shutterstock/Annette Shaff; **54t** Shutterstock **54b** Shutterstock/Roman Sigaev; **55t** Animal Photography/ Barbara O'Brien; **55b** iStock/Paul Tessier; **56t** Warren Photographic/Jane Burton; **56c** Shutterstock/A. Annal; **57b** Warren Photographic/Jane Burton; **58** Warren Photographic/Jane Burton; **59t** iStock/P. K. Photos; **59b** iStock/Lissart; **60t** DK Images/Tracy Morgan; **60b** DK Images/Jane Burton; **61** Shutterstock/Erik Lam; **62** Warren Photographic/Mark Taylor; **63t** Shutterstock/Michael Pettigrew; **63b** Shutterstock/Susan Schmitz; **64c** Warren Photographic/Jane Burton; **64b** Warren Photographic/Jane Burton; **65t** Shutterstock/Willee Cole; **65b** Shutterstock/Kudrashka-a; **66** Shutterstock/Erik Lam; **67t** Shutterstock/Eric Isselée; **67b** Shutterstock/Eric Isselée; **68t** Shutterstock/Elliot Westacott; **68c** Shutterstock/Ljupco Smokovski; **69** Warren Photographic/Jane Burton; **70t** Shutterstock/Margo Harrison; 70b Shutterstock/Rolf Klebsattel; **71** Shutterstock/Margo Harrison; **72** Shutterstock/Anne Kitzman; **73t** iStock/Revart; **73b** Shutterstock/Maksym Gorpenyuk; **74–75** Shutterstock/Erik Lam; **76tc** Warren Photographic/Jane Burton; **76b** Warren Photographic/Jane Burton; **77** Warren Photographic/Jane Burton; **78** Warren Photographic/Jane Burton; **79t** Shutterstock/ Suponev Vladimir; **79b** Shutterstock/Tom Prokop; **80** Shutterstock/Paul Cotney; **81t** Shutterstock/Nikolai Tsvetkov; **81b** Shutterstock/Liliya Kulianionak; **82tl** Warren Photographic/Jane Burton; **82c** Warren Photographic/Jane Burton; **83t** Warren Photographic/Jane Burton; **83b** Animal Photography/Paul Cotney; **84t** Shutterstock/ Eric Isselée; **84b** Warren Photographic/Jane Burton; **85t** Shutterstock/Anyka; **83b** Shutterstock/Willee Cole; **86** Shutterstock/Russ Beinder; **87t** iStock/Carrick4; **87b** Shutterstock/Chris Howey; **88tl** Shutterstock/H. D. Connelly; **88b** Getty/Cavan Images; **89t** Corbis/Michael Kloth; **89b** Warren Photographic/Jane Burton; **90b** Shutterstock/Eric Isselée; **90c** Corbis/John Madere; **91** iStock/Iculizard; **92** Warren Photographic/Jane Burton; **93t** Warren Photographic/Jane Burton; **93b** Warren Photographic/Jane Burton; **94** Warren Photographic/Jane Burton; **95t** Shutterstock/Erik Lam; **95b** Warren Photographic/Mark Taylor; **96t** Warren Photographic/Jane Burton; **96cb** Warren Photographic/Mark Taylor; **97t** iStock/J. Bryson; **97b** iStock/J. Terry; **98t** Warren Photographic/Jane Burton; **98b** Warren Photographic/Chris Howey; **99** Shutterstock/Warren Goldswain; **100** Warren Photographic/Mark Taylor; **101t** Animal Photography/Barbara O'Brien; **101b** Corbis/Moodboard; **102–103** Warren Photographic/Jane Burton; **104** Shutterstock/Eric Isselée; **105t** Animal Photography/Dorien Brouwers; **105b** DK Images/David Ward; **106** Shutterstock/Paul Cotney; **107t** Warren Photographic/ Jane Burton; **107br** Warren Photographic/Jane Burton; **107bl** iStock/Phototalk; **108** iStock/GlobalP; **109t** Warren Photographic/Kim Taylor; **109b** Shutterstock/Simone van den Berg; **110** Warren Photographic/Jane Burton; **111** Shutterstock/Willee Cole; **112** Warren Photographic/Jane Burton; **113** Shutterstock/Eric Isselée; **114b** Warren Photographic/Jane Burton; **115t** Warren Photographic/Jane Burton; **116b** Warren Photographic/Mark Taylor; **116t** Shutterstock/D. M. V. Photos; **117** Shutterstock/Jacqueline Abromeit; **118** iStock/Ryan J. Lane; **119t** iStock/Ilbusca Photography; **119b** iStock/Mark Hatfield; **120** Animal Photography/Sally Anne Thompson; **121t** Warren Photographic/Jane Burton; **121cb** Warren Photographic/Jane Burton; **122** Shutterstock/Erik Lam; **123t** Shutterstock/Holly Kuchera; **123b** Shutterstock/Eric Isselée; **124** Warren Photographic/Jane Burton; **125** Warren Photographic/Jane Burton; **126** DK Images/David Ward; **127** Getty/Mark Scroggins; **128c** Warren Photographic/Jane Burton; **129b** Warren Photographic/Mark Taylor; **130t** Shutterstock/Willee Cole; **130b** Shutterstock/Jean Frooms; **131t** iStock/Lillis Photography; **131b** Getty/Tracy Morgan; **132–133** DK Images/David Ward; **134** Animal Photography/Sally Anne Thompson; **135ct** Shutterstock/Erik Lam; **135b** Shutterstock/Dog Box Studio; **136** DK Images/Tracy Morgan; **137** Animal Photography/Tetsu Yamazaki; **137br** Animal Photography/Eva-Maria Krämer; **138–139** Warren Photographic/Jane Burton; **139tr** Animal Photography/Barbara O'Brien; **140–141c** Animal Photography/Barbara O'Brien; **141tl** Shutterstock/Boris Djuranovic; **141b** Shutterstock/Eric Isselée; **142tl** Shutterstock/Eric Isselée; **142br** Shutterstock/Eric Isselée; **143cr** Animal Photography/Tetsu Yamazaki; **143bl** Shutterstock/Big Zen Dragon; **144tr** Warren Photographic/ Jane Burton; **144bl** Shutterstock/Chris A. Anderson; **145t** Shutterstock/Katrina Leigh; **145b** Animal Photography/Tetsu Yamazaki; **146t** Shutterstock/Tkemot; **146b** Animal Photography/Barbara O'Brien; **147t** Shutterstock/Eric Isselée; **147b** Shutterstock/Eric Isselée; **148–149c** Animal Photography/Tetsu Yamazaki; **148b** Shutterstock/Eric Isselée; **149tr** Shutterstock/Erik Lam; **150t** Shutterstock/Eric Isselée; **150b** Shutterstock/Eric Isselée; **151** Animal Photography/David Jensen; **152** Warren Photographic/ Jane Burton; **153t** Shutterstock/EcoPrint; **153b** Shutterstock/Gelpi; **154t** Animal Photography/Tetsu Yamazaki; **154b** Shutterstock/Jean Frooms; **155t** Shutterstock/Erik Lam; **154–155c** Warren Photographic/Jane Burton; **156–157c** Shutterstock/Nikolai Tsvetkov; **156b** Shutterstock/Sparkling Moments Photography; **157** iStock/ Figure8Photos; **158bl** Warren Photographic/Jane Burton; **158–159c** Animal Photography/Barbara O'Brien; **159t** Shutterstock/Frederic Prochasson; **159cr** Corbis/Tim McGuire; **160** DK Images/Tracy Morgan; **161t** Shutterstock/Erik Lam; **161b** Shutterstock/Plavevski; **162** Shutterstock/Eric Isselée; **163t** Getty/U. S. Navy; **163b** iStock/ James Brey; **164** Ardea/John Daniels; **165b** DK Images/Dave King; **165t** iStock/Sadeugra; **166** Animal Photography/Barbara O'Brien; **167t** Shutterstock/J. Paget, R. F. Photos; **167b** Shutterstock/Dennis Sabo; **171** Shutterstock/Marika Wisniewska; **173** Shutterstock/Eric Isselée